Tentacles Longer Than Night

[Horror of Philosophy, vol. 3]

T0159475

Tentacles Longer Than Night

[Horror of Philosophy, vol. 3]

Eugene Thacker

Winchester, UK
Washington, USA

First published by Zero Books, 2015
Zero Books is an imprint of John Hunt Publishing Ltd., Laurel House, Station Approach,
Alresford, Hants, SO24 9JH, UK
office1@jhpbooks.net
www.johnhuntpublishing.com
www.zero-books.net

For distributor details and how to order please visit the 'Ordering' section on our website.

Text copyright: Eugene Thacker 2014

ISBN: 978 1 78279 889 7

A CIP catalogue record for this book is available from the British Library.

Design: Stuart Davies

Printed and bound by CPI Group (UK) Ltd, Croydon, CR0 4YY

We operate a distinctive and ethical publishing philosophy in all
areas of our business, from our global network of authors to
production and worldwide distribution.

CONTENTS

Also in the series:

1. Tentacles Longer Than Night

The Vast and Seething Cosmos (Poe, Lovecraft). In 1843, Edgar Allan Poe published his short story "The Black Cat." It opens with the following passage:

> For the most wild, yet most homely narrative which I am about to pen, I neither expect nor solicit belief. Mad indeed would I be to expect it, in a case where my very senses reject their own evidence. Yet, mad am I not – and very surely do I not dream. But to-morrow I die, and to-day I would unburthen my soul. My immediate purpose is to place before the world, plainly, succinctly, and without comment, a series of mere household events. In their consequences, these events have terrified – have tortured – have destroyed me. Yet I will not attempt to expound them. To me, they have presented little but Horror – to many they will seem less terrible than *baroques*. Hereafter, perhaps, some intellect may be found which will reduce my phantasm to the common-place – some intellect more calm, more logical, and far less excitable than my own, which will perceive, in the circumstances I detail with awe, nothing more than an ordinary succession of very natural causes and effects.[1]

An opening that is, perhaps, unparalleled in horror literature. Poe prepares us to expect something incredible, but without giving us any particular clue as to what that will be. Regardless of what follows, we as readers are primed to experience something indefinite, something the narrator does not – or cannot – define in any concrete way. All that we know from this opening is that what the narrator has witnessed seems to defy all rational explanation. The narrator even questions himself – was it a dream, a drunken hallucination, insanity itself? This self-interrogation (before the narrative has even begun) raises the stakes of the story. Whatever abstract horror has happened, it cannot be explained by the narrator. And yet, it must be explained, *there must be an explanation*. The narrator is so committed to this notion that he is willing to question his own sanity so that the "Horror" can be explained. And, the narrator continues, if I can't explain it then there must be someone else who can. In lieu of this, he can only hope that someone else (doubtless we, the "dear readers") will come along and provide an explanation, some explanation, any explanation.

What cannot be accepted is that something happened for no reason. But this event is not just an everyday event. It has the character of being out-of-place, of not fitting into our everyday or even scientific modes of explaining the world. It threatens the order of things produced by we human beings, living human lives in a human world largely (we presume) of our own making. That something, that event, might threaten this order of things, *and that it would happen for no reason* – this is, for the narrator of "The Black Cat," the real horror. It is a thought that cannot be accepted, without either abandoning reason and descending into the abyss of madness or making the leap of faith into religion and mysticism. It is as if, before Poe's story has even begun, the horror tale itself is in a state of crisis, the narrator nearly having a breakdown before us, only able to communicate himself in vague terms and uncertain utterances.

The story does go on, however. And through the narrator's point of view, we encounter a string of events that involves depression, alcoholism, a fire, a tavern, a noose, strange portents, the cellar of a house, murder, inhuman wailing, and two black cats, which may or may not be the same cat reincarnated. "The Black Cat" gives us a classic example of an unreliable narrator, who suggests strange events that may be supernatural, but which are, at the same time, undercut by the narrator's mental instability. Was that shadowy burn-mark on the wall really an image of the deceased cat, or was our unreliable narrator just "seeing things"? Is the white patch on the black cat's chest changing shape and forming the image of a gallows, or has the narrator had too much to drink? These and other conundrums produce the kind of suspenseful *frisson* for which Poe is well known. And the wavering of the story, between "it's all in his head" and "it really happened" is also a hallmark not only of Poe's work, but of the entire tradition of supernatural horror.

So much is this a cornerstone of supernatural horror that, almost a century later, H.P. Lovecraft could open his story "The Shadow Out of Time" with the following:

> After twenty-two years of nightmare and terror, saved only by a desperate conviction of the mythical source of certain impressions, I am unwilling to vouch for the truth of that which I think I found in Western Australia on the night of July 17-18, 1935. There is reason to hope that my experience was wholly or partly a hallucination – for which, indeed, abundant causes existed. And yet, its realism was so hideous that I sometimes find hope impossible. If the thing did happen, then man must be prepared to accept notions of the cosmos, and of his own place in the seething vortex of time, whose merest mention is paralysing. He must, too, be placed on guard against a specific lurking peril which, though it will never engulf the whole race, may impose monstrous and unguessable horrors upon certain venturesome members of it. It is for this latter reason that I urge, with all the force of my being, a final abandonment of all attempts at unearthing those fragments of unknown, primordial masonry which my expedition set out to investigate.[2]

Lovecraft's narrator expresses much of the same disbelief and commitment to explanation that Poe's narrator does. But Lovecraft does give us more details. The narrator of "The

Shadow Out of Time" is one Nathaniel Wingate Peaslee, Professor of Political Economy at Miskatonic University and resident of Arkham, Massachusetts. We are also given concrete references to a date ("July 17-18, 1935"), a place ("Western Australia"), and, it seems, an object of the horror ("unknown, primordial masonry"). And yet we know nothing more than we did with "The Black Cat." Peaslee's narrative is just as confused, uncertain, and delirious as that of the narrator of "The Black Cat." Like the latter, Peaslee also questions himself, more than willing to attribute what he witnessed to hallucination or even insanity.

And yet, what is more terrifying that insanity is the possibility that "it" really happened. This is a crucial twist in both Poe's and Lovecraft's stories – what is horrific is not that one is insane, but that one is *not* insane. At least if one is insane, the strange, terrifying "it" can be explained in terms of madness, delirium, melancholia, or in terms of clinical psychopathology. But other option is, for Peaslee, unacceptable: "If the thing did happen, then man must be prepared to accept notions of the cosmos, and of his own place in the seething vortex of time, whose merest mention is paralysing." The stakes are, perhaps, even higher than they were with "The Black Cat," for here Lovecraft situates human beings and human knowledge within the vast, "seething vortex of time" and the anonymous, "lurking peril" that portends only "monstrous, unguessable horrors" for the human race.

The dilemma for Peaslee (again, before the story has even begun) is this: either I stick to what I know, and forcibly reduce everything to illusion (madness, drugs, temporary insanity, whatever), or I accept what is real, but then because this is so alien to what I know, then I really know nothing at all. This notion – that I cannot accept what is real – is the core of this type of story that Lovecraft himself referred to as "supernatural horror."[3] As with "The Black Cat," the result is a threat, one that promises to destabilize our most basic presuppositions about the world (especially the world for us as human beings), but it is also a threat that is unspecific (though "cosmic"). In "The Shadow Out of Time" horror is not just the horror of fear or of a physical threat, but an indefinite horror. Language falters, as does thought.

This is all in that opening paragraph. But "The Shadow Out of Time" also goes on. In the process we are witness to other, menacing dimensions, ancient archaeological findings, telepathic possessions, and fleshy geometries so ancient they are alien, all of it undermined by Peaslee's own incredulity towards the reality that he cannot accept. Again, the horror of philosophy. In this sense stories like "The Black Cat" and "The Shadow Out of Time" sit squarely between those stories that do have rational explanations (for instance, mesmerism in "The Facts in the Case of M. Valdemar" or the fourth dimension in "The Dreams in the Witch House"), and those that appear to verify the supernatural (for instance, resurrection in "Morella" and "The Outsider"). As different as they are, Poe's tales and those of Lovecraft deal in some way with what is essentially a philosophical problematic, well-known to students of Aristotelian logic – that everything that happens has a reason for happening, and can thus be explained. This "principle of sufficient reason" not only grounds philosophical inquiry, but some of the basic principles of story-telling as well, especially in those genres – such as horror – where what is often at stake is the verification of something strange actually existing.

*

Horror of Philosophy. It's all in your head. It really happened. These mutually exclusive statements mark out the terrain of the horror genre. And yet, everything interesting happens in the middle, in the wavering between these two poles – a familiar reality that is untenable, and an acknowledged reality that is impossible. The literary critic Tzvetan Todorov calls this ambiguous zone "the fantastic," in his seminal work of same name. Discussing Jacques Cazotte's 18th-century occult tale *Le Diable amoureux*, Todorov provides a definition of the fantastic:

> In a world which is indeed our world, the one we know, a world without devils, sylphides, or vampires, there occurs an event which cannot be explained by the laws of this same familiar world. The person who experiences the event must opt for one of two possible solutions: either he is the victim of an illusion of the senses, of a product of the imagination – and laws of the world then remain what they are; or else the event has indeed taken place, it is an integral part of reality – but then this reality is controlled by laws unknown to us.[4]

While Todorov is primarily concerned with analyzing the fantastic as a literary genre, we should also note the philosophical questions that the fantastic raises: the presumption of a consensual reality in which a set of natural laws govern the working of the world, the question of the reliability of the senses, the unstable relationships between the faculties of the imagination and reason, and the discrepancy between our everyday understanding of the world and the often obscure and counterintuitive descriptions provided by philosophy and the sciences. The fork in the road is not simply between something existing or not existing, it is a wavering between two types of radical uncertainty: either demons do not exist, but then my own senses are unreliable, or demons do exist, but then the world is not as I thought it was. With the fantastic – as with the horror genre itself – one is caught between two abysses, neither of which are comforting or particularly reassuring. Either I do not know the world, or I do not know myself.

Given the degree of self-reflexivity in genre horror today, we are, most likely, well aware of the various ruses through which the fantastic is introduced. Contemporary films such as *Cabin in the Woods* (2012) self-consciously play upon genre conventions as well as on our expectations as viewers. If a character sees something supernatural we immediately question them: was it a dream, are they on drugs, are they insane, or is it simply a bit of visual trickery? We are also aware of how quickly an apparently supernatural event in a horror story – such as the actual existence of vampires or zombies – gets recuperated into the understanding of how the world works, thereby becoming quite unexceptional and normal – even banal. Biology, genetics, epidemiology, and a host of other explanatory models are employed in providing rational explanations for vampiric bloodlust or the resurrection of zombie flesh. Either way, the hesitation before the fork in the road is quickly resolved. Only in that brief moment of absolute uncertainty – when both options seems equally plausible and implausible, when neither thought can be accepted or rejected, when everything can be explained and nothing can be explained – only in that moment do we really have this horror of philosophy, this questioning of the principle of sufficient reason. It is for this reason that Todorov qualifies his definition by stating that the "fantastic occupies the duration of this uncertainty."[5]

This uncertainty lasts but a moment; the dilemma it presents to us is between two mutually exclusive, though equally plausible options. Rare are the works of horror that can sustain the fantastic for their entirety. An exception is the well-known *Twilight Zone* episode "Nightmare at 20,000 Feet," which aired in 1963. Based on a short story by Richard Matheson of the same title, it is a study in the fantastic, and manages to sustain that uncertainty up until its end. The episode centers on the character of Robert Wilson (played by the inimitable William Shatner), a very normal, middle-aged businessman and husband, who is returning home from the hospital after a mental breakdown. "Bob" (as he is referred to in the episode), along with his wife

Julia, are boarding an airplane as the episode begins. In the austerity that has become a hallmark of the original *Twilight Zone* episodes, the entirety of the episode takes place within this airplane. Pensive and nervous, Bob is continually reassuring himself that he is cured, and that everything will be alright. Thus, before anything strange has even happened, we have been primed to "explain" anything unusual in light of Bob's mental illness. En route, the airplane enters a storm. Unable to sleep, Bob glances out the window. Unsure of what he sees, he looks closer, and we as viewers see what he sees: a strange, grotesque creature outside, hunched over the wing. Director Richard Donner uses juxtapositions of shot and reverse-shot to let us "see" through Bob's eyes, while also judging him with suspicion, knowing what we do of his mental illness. Through a series of tension-filled events, Bob becomes convinced (as perhaps we do as viewers) that there is a strange creature on the wing of the plane. To our frustration, however, Bob fails to convince his wife or the flight engineer – each time he attempts to draw their attention to it, the creature vanishes. We, along with Bob, are deprived of the sole verification of the actual existence of the creature – that others witness it as well, and that it is not merely the product of an over-active imagination.

And yet, while we may attribute the creature to Bob's mental illness (as Julia and the flight engineer do), we as viewers also see the creature. We are the "others" that bear witness to the fantastic event, though we are not, of course within the story world. This play between the "uncanny" (Bob is hallucinating) and the "marvelous" (the actual existence of the creature) continues throughout the episode. Things become even more tense when Bob sees that the creature is pulling apart the wing of the airplane. In a climactic scene Bob takes matters into his own hands, attempting to kill the creature, opening the emergency escape hatch and forcing the plane down. Exhausted, delirious, and bound to a stretcher, Bob is taken out of the plane to an ambulance (interestingly, the director uses a point-of-view shot here, as we look up and see a policeman looking down at us). As the camera zooms out from the airplane, a final shot reveals something strange, which forces us to accept Bob's claims as true. This apparently objective evidence of a "something" out there returns us again to the fantastic, caught between the uncanny and the marvelous.

Contemporary works of horror have taken up techniques for sustaining the fantastic that we see in authors like Matheson. An example is the film *A Tale of Two Sisters* (2003), made by South Korean director Ji-woon Kim. The film is loosely based on a well-known Korean folktale, "Janghwa, Hongryeon," which tells the story of two sisters, Janghwa ("Rose Flower") and Hongryeon ("Red Lotus"), the death of their mother, an evil stepmother's plotting, the strange murders of the sisters, and their return as ghosts that haunt their family and the town in which they live. Kim's film introduces us to the teenage sisters – Su-Mi and Su-Yeon – who are spending a vacation in a remote lakeside house with their father and stepmother. Eventually the family dynamics are revealed – the morose, passive father, the manipulative stepmother, and the sisters, one of them rebellious (Su-Mi) and the other timid (Su-Yeon). But, like "Nightmare at 20,000 Feet," the film opens in a sanitarium, as Su-Mi, slumped over a chair in white gown and long black hair, is being gently questioned by a doctor. Here again we are primed to suspect everything we see in terms of mental illness. Throughout the film – most of which takes place in the house – we witness the family drama between the sisters and their stepmother. Su-Mi has a series of disturbing dreams concerning her birth mother which blur the line between dream and reality.

A good part of *A Tale of Two Sisters* takes place within this realistic mode – though the lush, shadowy, mesmerizing cinematography gives even the "realistic" scene a hallucinatory feeling. These scenes are punctuated by the fantastic. At one point, family friends are visiting for dinner. When one of them inexplicably begins choking, she falls to the floor, and – still choking – sees something eerie and impossible beneath the kitchen counter. And yet, just when we expect the marvelous and the actual existence of the supernatural, the film turns again. The father, confronting the increasingly rebellious Su-Mi, attempts to explain to her that she is not well – suddenly the camera point of view shifts, and we as viewers suspect that Su-Mi has not been fighting with her stepmother, but with herself, acting out the role of her projected image of her stepmother. We are back to the uncanny. In a stark, mesmerizing, final scene, the real stepmother returns one night to the lakeside house. In the room where Su-Mi's mother had died, she witnesses something inexplicable. We are back to the fantastic, suspended between conflicting points of view and a series of impossible happenings.

The fantastic, then, is central to supernatural horror, though, as Todorov reminds us, the sorts of questions it poses can even undermine the genre itself. The fantastic may exist only briefly, or it may span the duration of the story itself. While the questions that the fantastic poses may be answered, moving us towards either the "uncanny" or the "marvelous," the questions themselves are more important than the answers – they are moments in which everything is up for grabs, nothing is certain, the ground giving way beneath our feet. Within the genre conventions of horror, the fantastic interjects questions that are, in another guise, philosophical questions.

With this in mind, we can suggest a different way of approaching the horror genre. Certainly the products of genre horror – given its low-brow history – are more often regarded as entertainment, and this is, to be sure, an important part of the genre. But there is no reason why we cannot, at the same time, appreciate the works of genre horror for these sorts of – dare we say – philosophical questions they raise, as well as the ways in which they question our presumption to know or understand or explain anything at all. Hence the title of this series – *Horror of Philosophy* – which has several meanings. Certainly any reader of difficult philosophy books will have experienced their own kind of horror of philosophy, reinforced today by public intellectuals, who most often use philosophy as a smokescreen for selling self-help books and promoting the cult of the guru.

But the title also means a certain way of approaching the horror genre, which inverts the idea of a "philosophy of horror," in which philosophy explains anything and everything, telling us that a horror films means this or that, reveals this or that anxiety, is representative of this or that cultural moment that we are living in, and so on. Perhaps genres such as the horror genre are interesting not because we can devise ingenious explanatory models for them, but because they cause us to question some of our most basic assumptions about the knowledge-production process itself, or about the hubris of living in the human-centric world in which we currently live.

In the second volume of this series – *Starry Speculative Corpse* – I proposed "mis-reading" works of philosophy as if they were works of horror. There we saw how each philosophy contains a thought or set of thoughts that it cannot think without risking the integrity of the philosophical endeavor itself. In this volume – *Tentacles Longer Than Night* – I would propose we do the same. Except that, in this case, we will be mis-reading works of horror as if they were works of philosophy. What if we read Poe or Lovecraft as philosophers rather than as writers of short stories? What if we read Poe or Lovecraft as non-fiction? This means that the typical concerns of the writer or literary critic – plot, character, setting, genre, and so on – will be less relevant to us than the ideas contained in the story – and the central thought that runs through much of supernatural horror is the limit of thought, human characters confronted with the limit of the human. In short, we will be taking the horror genre as being essentially idea-driven, rather than plot-driven (and this certainly bears itself out in writers such as Lovecraft and his circle). In fact, I would even go so far as to say that what is unique about the horror genre – and particularly supernatural horror – is its indifference to all the accoutrements of human drama. All that remains is the fragmentary and sometimes lyrical testimony of the human being struggling to confront its lack of "sufficient reason" in the vast cosmos. And even this is not sufficient.

*

On Supernatural Horror (A Personal History). Granted, I may adopt such a method of reading, but that still doesn't guarantee that I will necessarily like what I'm reading. After all, there's no accounting for taste. At the same time, it would be misleading for me to say that this interest – in reading horror as philosophy – comes from a purely academic or scholarly impulse. There are personal motives too. Although I wouldn't say I'm your typical horror fan (whatever that is). I have my likes and dislikes certainly. I never tire of watching Argento's *Suspiria* or Kobayashi's *Kwaidan*, and no matter how many times I teach Algernon Blackwood's "The Willows" I'm always mesmerized by the lyrical and slightly dazed descriptions of the seemingly alive, hushed movement of the willows as they seem to imperceptibly move closer towards the narrator. Do those choices – rather than, say *True Blood* or *Walking Dead* or *Saw 3D* – make me a horror fan, or not? And if I consider Bergman's *Through a Glass Darkly* a horror film? If I consider Baudelaire's *Les Fleurs du mal* as important to the genre as Shelley's *Frankenstein* or Stoker's *Dracula*?

Such questions are, perhaps, not worth trying to answer. What I can offer is this short anecdote. When I was younger I was not an avid reader. Strange thing for a recovering English major to say, perhaps. I blame society; I grew up in the era of cable TV, home videos, and video games, so reading was, at best, something one had to do for school. But I also grew up around books and music, especially books, stacked row upon row in my father's studio. For my birthday one year my parents gave me an illustrated edition of Poe's stories. I recall reading "The Pit and the Pendulum" and finding it unlike anything I had read before. Part of the reason was that most of the story is virtually without plot. We as readers are simply dropped into this strange, dark, otherworldly scene with a sole character and an anonymous, swaying blade. We know nothing of who the character is, why he is there, where he is, if any of this is even really happening, or if it is a mere dream or hallucination. It is only at the very end of the story, in the last few lines, that we learn the character is being subject to torture by the Inquisition. But everything up until that point is strangely un-moored from the usual stuff of narrative fiction. Poe had written an *abstract horror* story, a study, a thought-piece, a meditation on finitude, time, and death.

This is of course one stock-and-trade interpretation of the story, but for me, at that time, it suddenly revealed something about the horror genre I had not expected: that the horror genre is as much driven by ideas as it is driven by emotions, as much by the unknown as by fear. A few years later, I discovered some of the Ballatine "Adult Fantasy" editions of Lovecraft on the bookshelf. I had the same revelation in reading "The Colour Out of Space": the characters in the story are confronted with something utterly inhuman and unknown, something that exists but at some other level where our senses are barred from access. The horror came not from what you saw, but from what you couldn't see, and even beyond that, what you couldn't fathom, what you couldn't think.

This was not limited to literature, either. Again, I grew up in an era when the low-budget horror film was big business, and so yes, I saw *Halloween*, *Friday the 13th*, *Return of the Living Dead*, and the rest. But on Sunday afternoons one of the local TV stations would show old horror films produced by Hammer Studios (many of them starring Christopher Lee and Peter Cushing), as well as Roger Corman's Poe adaptions produced for American International Pictures (many of them starring Vincent Price). What Corman did with the film images, Poe had done with language. The eerie opening of *The Pit and the Pendulum* is matched only by the closing scenes of the painterly, Piranesi-esque labyrinths of caves and tunnels. Almost a third of *The Masque of the Red Death* is devoted to a totally plot-less series of scenes that take place in strange, abstract, monochromatic rooms that reflect the moods of the characters. Again, abstract horror, idea-driven.

*

I Can't Believe What I See, I Can't See What I Believe. Re-reading some of these works today, what I find the most appealing is the way they can be read on different levels. This is a cliché, I know, but it is the thing that keeps me coming back to certain works (and not others…). Literary critics typically refer to this as allegory. When Dante, for instance, is taken by his guide Virgil on a tour of Hell, Purgatory, and Heaven, he undertakes a journey that is both real and symbolic, literal and allegorical. In the *Inferno*, we as readers are to understand that Dante really does encounter the Wood of Suicides, the dismembered Sowers of Discord, and the frozen, cavernous pit in which he finds a brooding Satan. But on the allegorical level Dante's journey is an interior one, which we understand as the spiritual journey of an individual. Dante himself was aware of this. In his writings he discusses allegory at length, noting both the different types of allegory (a frequently-used literary technique in the Middle Ages), as well as the way that his own *Divina Commedia* employs allegory. For instance, in a letter written to Cangrande della Scala, a nobleman and patron of the arts, Dante explains the use of allegory in his own work:

For the clarity of what will be said, it is to be understood that this work [the *Divine Comedy*] is not simple, but rather it is polysemous, that is, endowed with many meanings. For the first meaning is that which one derives from the letter, another is that which one derives from things signified by the letter. The first is called "literal" and the second "allegorical" or "mystical"... And although these mystical meanings are called by various names, in general they can all be called allegorical, inasmuch as they are different from the literal or historical. For "allegoria" comes the "alleon" in Greek, which in Latin is *alienum* [strange] or *diversum* [different].[6]

In this letter, Dante not only distinguishes the literal from the figurative, but he also notes the relationship between them. Although the allegorical derives from the literal, for Dante it is also more profound, ultimately having for him a mystical significance.

In his letter Dante goes on to suggest such a reading of the *Divine Comedy*: "The subject, then, of the whole work, taken in the literal sense only, is the state of souls after death, pure and simple. For on and about that the argument of the whole work turns... If, however, the work be regarded from the allegorical point of view, the subject is man according as by his merits or demerits in the exercise of his free will he is deserving of reward or punishment by justice."[7]

So, I continue to find the horror genre interesting not just on a literal level, but also allegorically. Now, as Dante knew, you can never really separate these from each other – the allegorical relies on the literal, just as the literal can be fleshed out or made more alluring by the allegorical. In other words, you *need* all those creatures, you need all the gory details of their metamorphoses, you need those tortured descriptions of a character's inner state as they confront something utterly alien – the allegorical level doesn't erase them; in fact, it brings them out even more. In a way, this runs counter to much literary criticism, enamored as it is of the higher levels of abstract, symbolic meaning, which quickly depart from the literal and rise up to those interpretive heights. But horror is "low." It is flesh and fluids, mud and material formlessness, inhuman matter of life reduced to primordial physics and cosmic dust. It is the *literalness* of horror that makes it horror; it is not "as if" an unnameable, tentacular, other-dimensional entity were feasting on your soul – it really is. And that is that. There is something about the literalness of horror that forces our language and our thought to stop dead in its tracks, a kind of tautology of "it is what it is" and yet the "it" remains indefinable, unmentionable, a thick and viscous and vaguely menacing "thing on the doorstep."

The allegorical is, then, in the service of the literal, and not the other way around. But what are these allegorical levels? How is the literalness of horror fleshed out in allegory? For me, there are several levels at work. First there is the literal level of the story itself, inclusive of the characters, the setting, strange happenings, and the conflict and resolutions that ensue. At its core are a set of feelings that we usually identify with horror stories – fear, terror, suspense, and the gross-out effect. But often we as readers or viewers get the sense that an author or director is out to explore "issues" – say, pertaining to mortality, morality, religion, science, politics, conflicts between "us" and "them," or what it means to be human. At this level, which starts to become allegorical, a horror story may explore very human issues through the lens of monsters, gore, and the supernatural, a story filled with human drama... in spite of the fact that such beings are very non-human. These are the sorts of paradoxes that allegory makes possible. How many viewers have identified with Boris Karloff's lumbering sensitive monster on seeing James Whales' production of *Frankenstein*? The same follows for modern examples, where our sympathies and antipathies drift and glide in different, often unexpected directions (a case in point is the sympathy for the zombies that is often evoked in George Romero's films).

These levels are not really separate from each other. A reader can be aware of the literal and allegorical levels at the same time – in fact, I would argue that the best horror fiction even demands this of us as readers. And this brings us to a third level at which genre horror operates – and that is the level of the horror genre itself. Some of the most interesting products of the horror genre are also about the genre itself. This is especially the case today, as horror film and TV programs increasingly rely on the viewer's knowledge of the genre and its rules, in order to play with or even break those rules. Some films make knowing, winking references within the film, others use game-like or puzzle-like structures to create suspense, and still others incorporate modern, technological devices into their stories, which serve as a commentary on the act of watching horror film itself.

Looking over some of the classics of horror fiction, one question that pops up again and again is whether the horror genre as a whole was to be identified with the supernatural. We are well aware of the gothic tradition of supernatural tales, as well as the creature-feature films of the 1930s and 1940s. However, since the days of films like *Psycho* and *Peeping Tom*, the horror genre has also explored psychological terrors, the terrors of our inner worlds. But if everything can be explained by science and psychology, then are we not in the adjacent genres of science fiction or the thriller? What then makes a work a part of the horror genre? Fans are still split on these sorts of questions, which will never be definitively answered. But if you grew up watching horror movies in the 1980s, you were well aware of this inner conflict, if only on a subconscious level. There were some films that were steeped in the supernatural, where the horror relied on what you didn't see (*The Shining, The Amityville Horror, Poltergeist*). Then there were those films that dispensed with the supernatural completely, the stalk-and-slash films that came out of the Italian *giallo* tradition and led to classics such as *Halloween* and *Friday the 13th*. In these films you saw everything, you even saw more than you wanted to see. Either the horror was what you couldn't see or the horror was what you could see all too well, either you had *supernatural horror* or you had *extreme horror*. (This dichotomy was evident in horror fiction too – on the one hand you had authors such as Ramsey Campbell and Thomas Ligotti, or you had authors associated with "splatterpunk"; and it continues to this day, for instance, in the dichotomy between "torture-porn" and J-horror films.) And even within a single film that conflict manifests itself – while Kubrick's *The Shining* is basically a haunted house story, it is precisely those elements that drive the main character to become a homicidal maniac (the supernatural becoming the natural); and we often forget that the masked killer in Carpenter's *Halloween* was referred to as "The Shape," taking on almost super-human qualities (the natural becoming supernatural).

These are, arguably, the two poles of the horror genre – extreme horror and supernatural horror, people doing things to people and non-people doing things to people, "I can't believe what I'm seeing" and "I can't see what I believe." Perhaps the horror genre is really defined in the space between these two poles, in the passages between them. This slipperiness has now become a hallmark of the genre, with authors such as Brian Lumley, Clive Barker, and China Miéville taking us from one pole to the other, and giving us rich, complex, story worlds that also bring together elements from several genres – fantasy, science fiction, the detective genre, historical fiction, and so on.

Is there another level beyond even this, a fourth allegorical level to the horror genre, one that actually takes us out of the world of story-telling itself? If so, perhaps that level would take us beyond the horror genre and into more general reflections on religion and religious experience. Now, by "religion" I do not simply mean the organized, institutional religion that we commonly associate with the monotheistic traditions of Judaism,

Christianity, and Islam. But that leaves a lot open. Contemporary philosophy of religion has had much to say on the boundary that divides religion from non-religion. Some argue for the value of alternative traditions, be they pagan or "Eastern," while others argue for a more complex and internally fraught understanding of monotheisms like Christianity, while still others argue for a sense of an everyday, polyglot spiritual awareness outside of any particular religious institution. But one commonality all these positions have is that they articulate a basic relationship between the human being and the limit of its capacity to adequately comprehend the world in which it finds itself. That experience of limits can be called "religious" (William James preferred the phrase "religious experience"), or, more narrowly, "mystical" (from the Greek adjective *mustikos*, or "hidden"). It broadly denotes an encounter with something essentially unknown, what theologian Rudolf Otto called "the numinous," an encounter with the "wholly other," a meeting with the horizon of our own understanding as human beings and the limit of thought this entails. That encounter may begin as the encounter with another person or other people, with a certain place or site, or with a book or a film or a work of music, or it might simply begin from a seemingly everyday, banal observation.

Whatever the case, this encounter with the unknown does not result in the kind of spectacular, beatific visions of light typically evoked by the word "mysticism." In fact, if one looks at, say, the tradition of Christian mysticism in the Middle Ages, what one finds are texts that are filled with ambiguity and ambivalence – evocations of "divine darkness," or "clouds of unknowing," or of the "dark night of the soul." They contain accounts of intense physical and spiritual suffering, of desert battles with legions of demons, of ecstasies and mortifications of the flesh, of passions so unhuman they can only come out as cries and sobs, of corpses happily entombed in an amorous embrace. If anything, we are presented with questions without answers, and problems without solutions. Should we say, then, that religious experience often runs counter to religion? But what counts as "experience" in this case, when we are at the limit of the senses and of thought? This is the "religious" allegory that I find so fascinating in the horror genre. But the 13th century context of, say, Dante's *Inferno* is markedly different from the late-20th century context of, say China Miéville's *Perdido Street Station*. Our contemporary horror stories are written in a world in which religious fanaticism routinely exterminates religious experience, a world in which scientific fanaticism explains and controls everything, a climatological world, after Nietzsche's "death of God," where there seems little faith, lost hope, and no salvation. And perhaps that is even another level at which the horror genre operates, if only obliquely. It is noticeable in those works that dare to delve into these other levels, especially this last level of a *religious horror*, where we pass beyond the pedantic world of humans doing bad things to other humans, and suddenly realize not only that the world remains indifferent to us, but that the world is and has always been mostly an inhuman world. Not a comforting thought. But then again neither philosophy, nor religion, nor horror, is meant to comfort.

2. Meditations on the Demonic

On Hell (Dante's Inferno). What the modern reader of Dante's *Inferno* discovers is not only an epic journey through the various regions of Hell, but a whole bestiary of strange landscapes and fantastical creatures that seem to be a blueprint for the horror genre. In fact – for better or worse – it is difficult not to read the *Inferno* as part of the horror genre. There is the torrential, swarming Circle of the Lustful, the burning bodies of the Heretics pouring out of their graves, the hybrid tree-corpses that populate the Forest of Suicides, the Plain of Thieves with limbs entwined by serpents, the anatomically dismembered Sowers of Discord – in addition to burning deserts raining flame, grotesque bogs of inertia, lakes of ice filled with corpses, a City of the Dead, rivers of boiling blood, stormy ravines and shadowy caverns, and a whole bestiary that includes mythological creatures such as Cerberus, the Furies, the Harpies, Centaurs, the Gorgon, giants, packs of demons, and of course, in the lowest circle, bestial, three-faced Satan, half-submerged in ice, weeping tears from six eyes, eternally flailing with six wings. If ever there was a sourcebook for the horror genre, then arguably this is it.

But it is also for this very reason that it can be difficult to appreciate the *Inferno*. When Dante wrote the *Commedia* in the early 14th century, he drew together a wide range of influences, from Greek mythology to Arabic philosophy to Christian theology, along with literary, historical, philosophical, and political references. We are so accustomed to films and TV shows featuring the living dead that it is difficult to appreciate the way in which Dante describes the City of Dis, a city of the dead in which a multitude of corpses – the Heretics – emerge from a field of open, fiery graves. The image is at once mythological, evoking the voyage to the underworld, and also political, at once a city, a cemetery, and a site of sovereign punishment. We have, perhaps, too much cultural baggage to really appreciate the *Inferno* in its historical, political, and cultural context.

At the same time, reading the *Inferno* retroactively as part of the horror genre allows us to take a step back from the intricacies and historical references that populate Dante's allegory. When we "zoom out" from the *Inferno*, one thing that makes itself clear is the way that it is structured, not only thematically but spatially. Everything is structured in this version of Hell, and, at the same time, everything flows. Contrary elements like fire and water merge into each other with the same effortlessness as the bodies of different creatures. The landscape and the climate of Hell is at once chaotic and ordered, just as the creaturely chaos within each circle is, at the same time, rigorously stratified in so many circles and layers.

That structure is well-known to any reader of the *Inferno*. Dante – who is both author of and character in the *Inferno* – finds himself lost in a dark forest, "midway along life's way." There he meets the epic poet Virgil, who guides him on a tour through Hell, Purgatory, and Paradise. As Dante (the character) and Virgil enter the gates of Hell, they see the inscription over the gates, which ends with the famous line: *Lasciate ogne speranza, voi ch'intrate*, "Abandon Every Hope, All You Who Enter."[8] Once inside, Dante, led by Virgil, passes through several "circles" of Hell, each of which contains a specific group of "shades" or souls of people who have committed particular wrongs for which they are being punished. Each circle corresponds to a specific type of wrong committed, and the entirety of Hell is therefore a kind of classification system of wrong-doings. Within each circle, the shades are punished according to the logic of the *contrapasso*, in which the punishment fits the crime (for instance, the second circle, the Circle of the Lustful, has groups of sinners continually blown this way and that by torrential winds, "winds" of desire). Each circle also contains a unique terrain, a unique climate, and various creatures, often borrowed from classical myth. The *Inferno* contains nine circles of Hell, which are divided among thirty-three cantos in the text, along with the prefatory canto. The nine circles roughly group into three clusters, according to the way they deviate from the perceived norms of human conduct:

Upper Hell (Circles I-V), dominated by an excess of passion.
Middle Hell (Circles VI-VII), dominated by perversions of passion or reason.
Lower Hell (Circles VIII-IX), dominated by an excess of reason.

Dante scholars conventionally refer to Upper Hell in terms of "incontinence" or the excesses of human emotion, to Middle Hell in terms of violence or perversions of the human nature, and Lower Hell in terms of deceit, fraud, or an excess of human intellect. This break-down generally follows Dante's appropriation of Aristotelian categories of the human faculties.

Thus the *Inferno* Hell is, first and foremost, a stratified domain, like so many geological layers of a fantastical world. Many modern editions of the *Inferno* provide diagrams which detail the various strata, since some of the circles – particularly the eighth and ninth circles – contain sub-circles, or *bolgia* ("ditches" or "trenches") which further stratify and classify the shades that populate Hell.[9] One of the most fascinating diagrams is the one by Wilfrid Scott-Giles, which accompanies Dorothy Sayers' celebrated 1949 translation of the *Inferno*.

I find this image fascinating in that it almost adopts an engineer's approach to Hell. The cut-away view clearly reveals the different strata of Hell, and the three-dimensional aspect gives a strong sense of the habitable worlds within worlds that is Dante's version of Hell. From a contemporary standpoint, this image also evokes a kind of game logic, as if Dante had, unwittingly, designed Hell as a video game – except that, strangely, the goal of the game would be to descend further into Hell rather

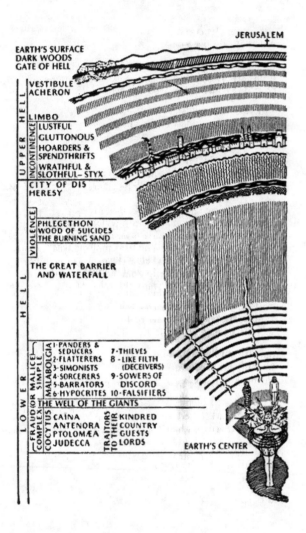

than to escape it.[10] Perhaps such a game would have a further rule – that, to advance to the next "level" of Hell, the player has to commit the sin of that particular circle. The more wrong the player does, the more points are awarded. (Indeed, within the narrative of the *Inferno* Dante the character does frequently commit the sins of the circle through which he is passing – for instance, in the Circle of the Wrathful Dante expresses hostility towards the shades that reach out for him.)

Interestingly, these types of images were common in early editions of the *Inferno*, stretching back to Dante's own time. Artists seemed to have gravitated towards this spatial, stratified aspect of the text, each devising their own way of visually representing Hell as a whole. Some opted for realistic depictions of particular scenes, while others adopted a more abstract, almost geometric method of representation, while still others offered top-down views of the circles of Hell. Many of the images produced during the Renaissance combined, in interesting ways, diagrammatic and pictorial methods of representation. The Benivieni edition of 1506 (also known as the "Giuntina" after its publisher Filippo Giunti), for instance, contains a number of cutaway diagrams in woodcut, such as the following:

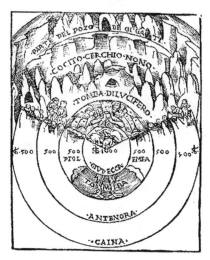

In tutti questi disegni (come uoi hauete potuto no
tare) miconomolte cose , et molte se nesono poste
quasi (come uulgarmente si dice) alla burchia
rispetto alla scarsita delli spatii et alla impossi
bilita della

This version, edited by the Florentine poet Girolamo Benivieni, was among the first editions of Dante's *Commedia* to provide a more "scientific" cosmology of Hell, Purgatory, and Paradise. Benivieni's edition was based on the work of Antonio Manetti –

mathematician, architect, and author – who undertook research into the worlds that Dante describes in his text, providing ways to render them visually. Manetti's research into Dantean cosmology was taken up by subsequent editors, and it is now standard in modern editions of Dante to include these kinds of summary diagrams. Such means of visually rendering Hell underscore the interplay between the micro-structure of the individual circles and the macro-structure of Hell itself; the correspondences between the individuated bodies within each circle and the collective, infernal "body" of Hell itself.

Such diagrams as this were, no doubt, intended as guides for the reader (thereby extending the allegorical aspect of Dante's text). They also underscore the spatial, architectonic design of Hell, with its myriad and chaotic scenes that are, at the same time, rigidly organized. This raises an important point about the *Inferno*: that, from this architectonic point of view, the tension central to Hell is the order of that which is disordered, the stratification of that which is de-stratifying, the classification of that which transgresses classification. These are central questions in political philosophy. How should things be structured such that they flow? What is the best way to order human beings and the culture which they have created? At what point does a political philosophy become a political theology?

Such questions dovetail on one of the oldest ideas in Western political philosophy, that of the body politic. Philosophers from Plato to Hobbes to contemporary political theorists have long drawn on the analogy between the individual human body and the collective body of society, whether to affirm the hierarchy of the body or to question it. If we take a look at Dante's *Inferno* in this way, what we find is that Dante provides us with an architectonic body politic, one in which landscapes, beasts, and various human bodies all come together to composed Hell itself. His general division of Upper, Middle, and Lower Hell is derived from Aristotelian ethics, which he then maps both spatially and corporeally.[11] Upper Hell, dominated by an excess of human emotion, is often correlated to the nether regions of the body, while Middle Hell, dominated by perversions of human nature, correlates to the heart, torso, and hands, and Lower Hell, dominated by an excess of reason, correlates to the "head" – both as the seat of intelligence and as the control center of the body.

In fact, we might describe the spatial design of the *Inferno* as an *architectonics of power*. It is hierarchical (the more serious the sins, the lower in Hell one is placed), but it is also a space of flux and flow (of the landscape, the different climates, the roving of various creatures, and the meandering human "shades" within it). As a whole the *Inferno* is a huge, cavernous structure often depicted as an inverted cone, each circle spiraling down to the center, the lowest point of Hell, where Satan sits, melancholy and frozen. The apex of Hell is nearly an inversion of the apex of a cathedral (which symbolizes, in turn, the theological "body" of the congregation, and which, in turn, configures the body as the "temple" of the soul). Thus an infernal cavern is presented in place of the divine temple. In short, in the *Inferno* Dante presents us with an inverted body politic, standing the body politic literally on its head.

Like any great systematizer, Dante's inferno does not form a perfect system, but contains many partial matches, subtle incongruities, and polysemic structures. Thus, while we can "apply" Dante's moral categories to the inferno as a whole physical structure, it is also important to note the resistances that each individual circle of Hell puts up against this holistic view. The human "shades" trapped within each circle long to escape their interminable punishment, even cursing the God that has put them there; the various creatures – demons, Furies, and Centaurs – likewise threaten to break out of their confined and functional roles; even the terrain of Hell, with its tempestuous storms, overflowing waters, and spreading cascades of fire, threatens to spill over into the other circles. In this sense, the "big" body politic that is the architectonics of the inferno must be read alongside the multitude of "little" bodies politic that populate and are part of the ceaseless turbulence that is the inferno itself.

In the *Inferno*, Dante inverts the traditional philosophical model of the body politic, standing it on its head. In doing this, we see different variations of the body politic theme, not as an ideal, coherent, and unified body politic, but as a series of dissolute, dismembered, and diseased bodies politic. In inverting the body politic, Dante shows us the body politic defined not by its ideal principles (the One, the whole, the head), but by those things that threaten and dissolve the body politic (the "creaturely" activities of chaotic flux and flow). In doing this, Dante reminds us of one the central issues in the body politic motif as it is developed in political philosophy: that the greatest threat to the coherence of the body politic comes from within it. We will see later on exactly how political philosophy manages this tension. For the time being, we can simply note the way Dante has not only written a work of "horror" but has also written a work that ties horror to political philosophy and political theology. In depicting Hell, Dante is led to invert the body politic, giving us not a political theology but instead a political demonology.

*

Digression on Hell. It is important to remind ourselves that each of the categories of sin (too much emotion, perversions of nature, too much reason) are not simply logical or conceptual categories, but are expressed through the architectonics that Dante puts forth. The problem of too much passion, which occupies Upper Hell, may be understood as uncontrolled appetite, the problem of nature uncontrolled, the domination of the animal life, the problem of "too much life." The most forceful expression of this is the famous second circle of the lustful (Canto V), depicted by

Dante as a swarming whirlwind of bodies, desire, and unbridled passion.

The problem of perversions of passion or reason occupies Middle Hell, and may be understood as perverted, monstrous behavior, the problem of the perversion of animal and human life, of natural reason, the problem of "abnormal life." Dante subdivides such perversions into three types: (i) violence against others (heresy, false doctrine), (ii) violence against the self (suicide), and (iii) violence against nature (usury, sodomy). The most interesting example of this abnormal life comes after Dante and Virgil pass through the gates of the City of Dis (Cantos VIII-XII). They encounter aberrations of life, beasts, and chimeras of all sorts: the living dead (IX, 106-133), the Furies (IX, 37-57), the Minotaur (XII), the Centaurs, the Harpies (XIII, 10-15), and the giant, monstrous Geryon (XVII). In addition, the punished sinners in Middle Hell also undergo strange metamorphoses. In the City of Dis the arch-heretics (those violent against others) are condemned to be living corpses; while in the Wood of Suicides (those violent against the self), human merges with plant, as the tortured bodies are twisted into trees; and the Burning Sand, the usurers and sodomites (those violent against nature) are stripped of everything except their bodies, a near echo of the living death of the arch-heretics. They are bodies without life, encircled by a river of boiling blood, the life-blood that is both extracted and externalized from the living body, and which confines them in a desert void of life.

In fact, it is this landscape of bare life that tells us the most about Middle Hell. We move from the city (which is really a city of graves, a necropolis), to the forest (which is really a dead forest), to the desert (whose life seems to have been extracted by the boiling blood. In this progression, we see the sequential extraction of natural, creaturely life from the human being, an extraction corresponding to the sinful acts that denigrate and pervert the "natural theology" of creaturely life. The city is only a necropolis, a city in ruins, while the forest is nearly barren and petrified, and the desert is, well, a desert.

But perhaps the most enigmatic figure of the bestial, abnormal life of Middle Hell comes at the end of Canto XIV, as Dante and Virgil are leaving the Burning Sand. Upon asking about the source of the river of blood that surrounds it, Virgil responds with a striking allegory about the "Old Man of Crete" (94-120). There Virgil tells about a giant, ancient man within Mount Ida in Crete, who "faces Rome as though it were his mirror." Combining references from Ovid and the Bible, Virgil describes the Old Man in terms that were, in the 14th century, becoming part of the political-theological vernacular of the body politic: the head and topmost region is made of gold, the torso or middle region of silver, and the lower regions of brass and iron (except for the right foot, which is of terra cotta). This giant, allegorical body shows some similarities to the body depicted in Plato's *Timeaus*, the "three-venter" body itself not unknown to the Greeks. But the body is everywhere cracked, and through the fissures tears drain down, gradually forming the mythical rivers of Acheron, Styx, and Phlegethon, and finally settling in the pool of Cocytus where Satan resides. If the Old Man is Christian Rome, and if this body is fractured from within, then the implication Dante seems to be drawing out here is that the body politic is showing signs of wear and tear. Not only is there a fissure between ecclesiastical and temporal authority (which Dante attempts to redress in his *De Monarchia*), but perhaps the very concept of the body politic is itself undergoing changes which threaten to fracture it from within. The question, then, would not only be about divine vs. secular authority, but about whether the body politic concept itself is a properly theological or political concept – an issue that is still not completely sorted even in later variants such as those by Hobbes.

Finally, the problem of too much reason, which covers Lower Hell, is appetite that is manipulated and used by reason and rendered deceitful, the problem of "instrumental life." Lower Hell is in many ways the most complex, containing as it does a veritable numerology of subdivisions and sins. The *Malbowges* contain ten sub-circles of "simple" fraud, including the sorcerers and thieves, while the circles around Cocytus contain more circles of "complex" fraud, including the different classes of traitors.

The sins of Lower Hell are also more complex. They involve not just uncontrolled appetite, and not just perverted nature, but the reasoned use of nature for malicious ends. This is, for Dante, the most dangerous of sins, but also the most sophisticated, the most "elevated." Animal, creaturely life is here not simply something that is embraced or obsessed over, but it is something that is amenable to reason and instrumentality – it is the creaturely life that can be used, rendered as a technics. The corporeal expression of this technics of life is the most forcefully and horrifically presented in the ninth *bolgia* where we encounter the Sowers of Discord (Canto XXVIII), and in the tenth, where we find the Falsifiers (Canto XXIX). In the former, the Sowers of Discord (which include Mohammed) are subject to the cruelest corporeal punishments: flaying, cutting, mutilation, and dismemberment abound here. But what makes these punishments so horrifying is precisely that they are punishments. They are carried out with an anatomical accuracy, according to the Biblical logic of the *contrepasso*, the "eye for an eye," the punishment fitting the crime. There is more than an echo here of the use of the cadavers of criminals or the poor for dissection in the early modern era; but it is also the heavily ritualized repetition of these anatomizations that is horrific.

Two examples show this specific, anatomical body politic. The first example is that of Mohammed, who is blamed for having split the unity of the Church, is himself ripped from hips to head. His body re-heals itself, only to have the punishment again inflicted. Here the implication is that the unified, hierarchical body of the Church is always threatened from within by those that diverge from its doctrine. If the Church is a single body politic, then any attempt to subvert the hierarchy (by creating new heads or limbs) can only destroy the body politic by dividing it. A second example comes at the end of the canto, with the figure of Bertran de Born, who, out of hubris, turned a young prince against his father. His punishment is decapitation, and to walk eternally holding his head by the hair. Here, Bertran is accused not only of turning the prince against the king, but of turning a son against a father. The body politic of the family is echoed in the body politic of the city-state (a very Aristotelian variant on the theme). And again the threat comes from within; the usurpation of the "head" (of family, of the city-state) can only end in the decapitation and death of the body politic altogether.

These two examples of Dante's anatomical body politic each emphasize a different part of the motif. The corporeal splitting of Mohammed stresses the unity of the body under a single head, while the decapitation of Bertran de Born stresses the singular unity of the head over the body. This anatomical body politic is further expanded in the following canto and the following *bolgia*, where we witness the various falsifiers each afflicted with diseases (including plague and leprosy). We have here a third aspect of the body politic, that of the diseased or "sick" body. Presumably, the Falsifiers' rumors circulate through the body politic, causing illness to the coherence and unity of the body politic itself. Communication, then, plays a central role is the spreading of such diseases. Language (*logos*) spreads throughout the body politic, and, like the other variants we've seen (Mohammed, Bertran), it also causes disease from within.

In the anatomical bodies politic presented in each of the sections of sinful activity (too much emotion, perversion of nature, too much reason), we see bodies that are at once individual bodies subjected to sovereign punishment, and a body politic that is dismembered, dissected, and diseased as a result of such acts of creaturely sin. If we take these two types of body politic that Dante presents in the *Inferno* together – the architectonic body politic (the "big" body) and the anatomical body politic (the "little" body) – we can discern an important relation between them. In the architectonic body politic, Dante presents us with an inversion of the body-as-temple metaphor, standing the body politic on its head, as it were. Here we have a redoubled analogy: the architectural building is analogized to the body, but then the body is then re-analogized, through the categories of creaturely sin, to actual anatomical bodies, that are finally also read as variants on the concept of the body politic, a concept that was itself undergoing many changes in the later Middle Ages.

*

Dead Tropes, Resurrected Bodies. To understand Dante's "political demonology" in the *Inferno*, we need to take a detour into the history of political philosophy. This will entail a brief overview, in which we can outline a series of basic principles concerning the body politic, principles which determine the *constitution* or composition of the body politic. At the same time, we will also note how this constitution tends to turn in on itself, the body politic devouring itself, and becoming defined by a *dissolution* or decomposition. Highlighting this aspect of the body politic concept will require paying attention to various ideas that are at once medical and theological, natural and supernatural, that pertain to the domain of the dead and the living dead.

One of the most familiar images of the body politic comes from Hobbes, who articulates that image through a language of natural law – illustrated in the famous frontispiece of *Leviathan* – an image of the body politic that is by turns mechanistic, vitalistic, and theological. A passage from the introduction deserves to be quoted in full, providing as it does a sort of compendium of the concept:

> For by art is created that great LEVIATHAN called a
> COMMONWEALTH, or STATE (in Latin CIVITAS), which is
> but an artificial man, though of greater stature and strength
> than the natural, for whose protection and defence it was
> intended; and in which the *sovereignty* is an artificial *soul*, as
> giving life and motion to the whole body; the *magistrates* and
> other *officers* of judicature and execution, artificial *joints*;
> *reward* and *punishment* (by which fastened to the seat of the
> sovereignty every joint and member is moved to perform his
> duty) are the *nerves*, that do the same in the body natural; the
> *wealth* and *riches* of all the particular members are the *strength*;
> *salus populi* (the people's safety) its *business*; *counselors*, by
> whom all things needful for it to know are suggested unto it,
> are the *memory*; *equity* and *laws*, an artificial *reason* and *will*;
> *concord, health*; *sedition, sickness*; and *civil war, death*. Lastly, the
> *pacts* and *covenants* by which the parts of the body politic were
> at first made, set together, and united, resemble that *fiat*, or the
> *let us make man*, pronounced by God in the creation.[12]

There are, certainly, many comments to make on this paragraph
alone, and one can easily trace a lineage that moves backward to
the vague naturalism of political theorists such as Bodin, Grotius,
and Althusius (the latter's notion of the *corpus symbioticum*
deserves more attention in this regard), and forward to the
organicism of Hegel, Rousseau, and Nietzsche. However the goal
here is not to provide anything like a comprehensive history of
the idea. Rather, we can pay particular attention to the literalness
of the body politic concept expressed in passages such as these
(passages that are likewise echoed in Hobbes' *De cive* and *The
Elements of Law*). To call the body politic concept a metaphor
doesn't quite do justice to the way a great number of political
treatises take the concept at face value. Again and again, we find

specific comparisons made between the human body and political order, as if the basis for legitimacy in the latter depended on the coherence of the understanding of the former.

The body politic concept is particularly literal in what are often said to be the two key moments in Western political thought concerning the concept: that of its formulation around the city-state or *polis*, most thoroughly expressed in Plato, and that of a reformulation and recapitulation in the medieval theological notion of the *corpus mysticum*, the mystical body of believers united in the larger "body" of Christ.

Medieval scholars such as Étienne Gilson have noted the debt medieval philosophy owes to antiquity, and the body politic concept owes the same debt. In Plato the concept is formulated at several points in the *The Republic*, in which Socrates proposes understanding justice in the individual by extrapolating from the *polis*, or the individual "writ large." Plato immediately provides us with the language through which the body politic concept is most often understood – that of medicine, health, and illness. Socrates argues that "health is produced by establishing a natural relation of control and subordination among the constituents of the body, disease by establishing an unnatural relation," wherefrom he then posits that "justice is produced by establishing in the mind a similar natural relation of control and subordination among its constituents, and injustice by establishing an unnatural one." The conclusion arrived at by Socrates?: "It seems, then, that excellence is a kind of mental health or beauty or fitness, and defect a kind of illness or deformity or weakness."[13]

The Platonic body politic gives us several ideas that are fundamental to the body politic concept. The language of medicine, health, and illness implies there is something human and living that is larger than the living human individual. At the same time, this large, living, and human thing must be understood through a logic of parts and wholes. The subsequent sections of the *The Republic*, in which the ideal *polis* is laid out, discuss the body politic not only in terms of health and illness, but also in terms of parts and wholes: the body politic in Plato is divided into three sections, the sovereign head (the reasoning part), auxiliaries and soldiers in the heart or chest (the impassioned part), and the peasantry and laypeople in the nether regions of the groin (the animal part). Plato's body politic must be read alongside *Timeaus* for the tripartite division of the body it proposes (a rigid corporeal organization of parts and wholes that is, arguably, deconstructed in *Parmenides*).

This scaling-up procedure is also found, as we've noted, in later antiquity and the Middle Ages. Its greatest formalization, however, comes in late-medieval Scholasticism, itself profoundly influenced by the writings of Paul, whose notion of the *corpus mysticum*, or the mystical body of Christ, introduced the language of community into the theological variants of the body politic concept: "The body is a unit, though it is made up of many parts; and though all its parts are many, they form one body... there should be no division in the body, but that its parts should have equal concern for each other. If one part suffers, every part suffers with it; if one part is honored, every part rejoices with it."[14] However, while Platonic hierarchy and Aristotelian naturalism provide the philosophical terms for the medieval body politic concept, the idea also takes new turns in its emphasis on spirit, the creature, and corporeality, on a body that is ensouled, living, and never quite dead. Scholastic philosophy "brought out with no less force," Gilson notes, "the necessary connection between faith in the resurrection of the body, and the philosophical thesis of the substantial unity of the human composite."[15]

Significant sections of late-medieval political treatises, including those of Aquinas, Dante, Marsilius of Padua, Nicholas of Cusa, and William of Ockham contain passages in which the anatomical human body is analogized – or, we might say, anatomized – point for point with the body of the Church, the State, or some mixture of both. Entire texts, such as John of Salisbury's remarkable *Policraticus*, are based on this kind of tabular matching between individual-natural and collective-political body. The head, the limbs, the torso, the feet, as well as an entire symbolics of the viscera – heart, brain, hands, genitals – are all offered up as functional parts within a greater whole. Though there were, of course, extensive debates about what kind of body this "whole" was, and, more importantly, what constituted the sovereign "head" of this body, the terms of the discussions remained focused on this conceptual movement between an anatomical, individuated human body and an equally anatomized, but collective, political body.

*

As Above, So Below. Contrary to the treatment it often receives, the analogy of the body politic does not neatly progress from a theological to a secular order, or from divine law to natural law. It is filled with incongruities, diversions, and proliferations that express nothing in common except a lack of consensus on what exactly is the best or most ideal body politic.

Rather than elaborate endless quotations that demonstrate the body politic concept, we can present four principles that delineate the challenge posed by the body politic concept to political philosophy. These principles suggest that our current discussions have not yet rid themselves of the categories of thought historically formulated through the lens of political theology. But, at the same time, new problematics have arisen, ones that refashion the old debates in novel ways.

We begin with a first principle: *The body politic is a response to the challenge of thinking about political order.* Put another way: a minimal congruity between order as natural and artificial (political) is the a priori of the body politic concept. Thus the body politic is a way of thinking about politics as a living, vital order. It is a living, vital *order* insofar as it is defined within an ontology of the one and the many, of wholes and parts, and of the relation between the natural and the artificial. And it is a *living, vital order* insofar as it posits a correlation between the natural world and political order, either to say that the natural world is divinely ordered (as we find in Augustine), or to argue that political order is built upon a "natural law" (as we find in Hobbes and Spinoza).

However, to simply posit politics as a certain combination of the living and the ordered is not enough, for it is the way in which this relation is formulated that is important. This takes place through a figure, one that presupposes a certain correlation between "life" and "politics." Thus, a second principle: *the foundation for the intelligibility of political order is based on an analogy between the body natural and the body politic.* The former is said to preexist the latter, and often serves as its model; it is essential that the latter governs, manages, and regulates the former. Moreover, the body natural is often taken as the basic, individuated, atomic unit of human life, which is then extrapolated to a meta-individuated level for collective political existence. In a sense, the challenge of political thought is the correlation between the body natural and the body politic, for the two never exactly coincide. The analogy, as analogy, presupposes fissures and incongruities – does the body politic have one head or two (spiritual and temporal)? Is it a single system or does it have systems-within-systems ("corporations," "councils")? Nevertheless, in the relation between the body natural and the body politic we see a set of general criteria: there is the criteria of unity, for the body politic must be "one," a unified, coherent political body, a unity within which all multiplicity is accounted for, the single that encompasses the plural.

There is also the criteria of hierarchy, for the body politic obtains unity through stratification, or a set of defined relations between the "members" or parts of the political body. For instance, the modern cluster of political concepts sovereign/people/multitude stresses the relation between "head" and "body," while the late-medieval cluster God/priesthood/ faithful stresses the sovereign place of "soul" in the body politic. In his masterful study of the body politic, Ernst Kantorowicz shows how, in the later Middle Ages, the figure guaranteeing the continuity of sovereign power shifts from a Christ-centered, to a Law-centered, and finally to a "polity-centered" notion of rulership: "Late mediaeval kingship, from whatever point of view it be considered, had become polity-centered after the crisis of the 13th century. The continuity, first guaranteed by Christ, then by the Law, was now guaranteed by the *corpus mysticum* of the realm which, so to speak, never died, but was 'eternal' like the *corpus mysticum* of the Church."[16]

Finally, in addition to unity and hierarchy, there is a criteria of centralization, or better still, a certain concern with the governance of the vital flows and circulations that mark what Aquinas refers to as the "life-giving spirit" of the body politic. Jacques Le Goff remarks on an underexplored tension in late-medieval conceptions of the body politic: that between the "head," which is, for thinkers such as John of Salisbury, connected to the nerves that move the body, and the "heart," connected to the veins and responsible for the distribution of blood throughout the body. Le Goff suggests that debates over spiritual versus temporal rule often played themselves out through a kind of visceral topology, in which the rule of nerves and the rule of blood are pitted against each other: "The centrality attributed to the heart expresses the evolution of the monarchical state in which the most important thing is the *centralization* that is taking place around the prince, not the vertical hierarchy expressed by the head..."[17]

These criteria – unity, hierarchy, and centralization – are coupled to a narrative form, one that articulates the "constitution" of the body politic, both in terms of an account of the origins (and thus the legitimacy) of the body politic, and also in terms of that which guarantees the coherence of the body politic through time. The body politic is therefore conserved through a narrative of constitution. The most well-known of such narratives is the one derived from natural right theory, encapsulated by Hobbes as the transition from the pre-political state of nature to the laying down of rights and the establishment of a commonwealth. But Plato, both in the *The Republic* and in *The Laws*, has already given us a narrative of constitution in the analogies that Socrates makes between the idea of justice in the individual and the idea of justice in the *polis*, or the individual "writ large," and both Augustine and Aquinas likewise provide narrative accounts of the necessity of the divine sovereign and the guarantee of order in the act of creation.[18]

All of this implies a thoroughly abstract model to which, of course, an actual political regime may or may not correspond. Even though the body politic concept may entail a narrative of constitution or origin, this in no way means that the concept of the body politic itself precedes an actual political regime. In fact, the opposite is often the case, which brings us to a third principle: *the body politic is expressed retroactively in the language of political theology*. The body politic analogy is employed in order to justify or legitimize a de facto political order – that is, to justify a particular ontological relation between "life" and "order."

The term "political theology" has been used in different ways by a number of political thinkers, including Walter Benjamin, Carl Schmitt and Jacob Taubes. Conceptually it refers to the embodiment of sovereignty, be it in a single ruler (the King, the Pope – the "head") or in some notion of the people (popular sovereignty, collective rule, religious community – the "body"). Historically political theology refers to the manifold relations between spiritual and temporal powers in theological, legal, and Scholastic discourse in the later Middle Ages.[19] But it also refers to the necessity of a sovereign power that is at issue in the modern debates over political theology. Schmitt's primary argument, that "all significant concepts of the modern theory of the state are secularized theological concepts," argues for the necessity of an exceptional sovereign since it is in the very nature of the political to be unable to legitimize authority except by reference to an outside source.[20] Taubes disagrees, for, though the Judeo-Christian tradition does emphasize a sovereign law, in the Pauline tradition it also emphasizes a notion of community and, perhaps, a more pluralistic rule: "Carl Schmitt thinks apocalyptically, but from above, from the powers; I think from below."[21]

A political theology of the body politic raises a number of issues that directly link ontological questions to political ones. One of the central issues here is the question of sovereignty, the question of who acts as the "head" of the body politic (or indeed, what counts as a "head" in the body politic). For Schmitt, there is a direct correlation between the miracle in theology and the exception in politics, the latter being simply a secularized version of the former. Just as the divine sovereign is not only capable of establishing the natural workings of things, but is also able to intervene in the natural workings of things to make exceptional (or rather, supernatural) decisions, so is the secular sovereign capable of claiming an exception to the rule. "Political theology" is this relation between miracle and exception, and it is this aporetic state of being inside and outside that forms the basis of Giorgio Agamben's arguments concerning sovereignty. In terms of the body politic concept, this means that the "head" is both a part of the body (forming a unified, whole body politic) and yet detached from the body (it rules the body and stands opposite it in the exception).

Another issue is the question of the "two natures," which is summarized by the German legal theorist Otto von Gierke: "Two necessary attributes are thus presented as determining the conception of the State. One is the existence of a society...

directed to the objects which compel man to live together: the other is the existence of a sovereign power... which secures the attainment of the common end."[22] At issue is not only the shape that sovereignty takes (who acts as "head"?), but the often divided relation between ruler and ruled, sovereignty and community, "head" and "body." Gierke's theory – influential on the work of Kantorowicz – situates the debates between spiritual and temporal powers within the framework or organicism. Gierke's *Political Theories of the Middle Age* suggests that the "organic theory of the State," encapsulated in the analogy of the body politic, is an attempt to resolve an irremediable gap between ruler and ruled, between sovereign and people, between head and body: "In all forms of State indifferently, a distinction was drawn between the Ruler and the body of the Ruled: the legal basis of the Ruler's authority was regularly ascribed to a previous devolution of its own authority by the body of the Ruled."[23]

These characteristics of the body politic, predicated as it is on a top-down model that emphasizes the rule of the "head" over the rest of the "body," may appear to us as a rigid and inflexible concept. In so far as the body politic concept serves to legitimize a given political order, this would not be far from the case. But it is also important to stress the many internal tensions, inconsistencies, and curious permutations that the body politic undergoes, especially in the context of political theology. Thus a fourth principle: *the body politic creates a logically coherent monstrosity*. This is not to say that the body politic – like Roberto Esposito's description of biopolitics – is, in an "immunitary" fashion, dependent on that which negates it. In many of the early modern debates, there is little concern for boundary management and forms of immunization. Rather, it suggests that the concept of the body politic, raised as it is to address a problem of political ontology, often entails the creation of aberrant logics – that is, modes of thinking that make sense logically but that result in an image of the body politic that can only be described as terato-logical. One sees such a monstrous logic in discussions over dual sovereignty, which result in a "two-headed" or bicephalic body politic, as seen in the political writings of Dante, Ockham, and Giles of Rome.[24] Limbs multiply or are cut off, the mouth and anus become mirrors of each other, and the lowest parts partake of the divine. As such, the body politic is not a single, unified concept but one that constantly rises, falls, and is brought back to life again. It is a concept predicated on variations, permuta-tions, and recombinations, like so many interchangeable anatomical parts. The debates of the preoccupied late-medieval Scholasticism were not simply debates over Church and State; they were a set of attempts to resolve the tension between "head" and "body," sometimes with rather bizarre, monstrous implica-tions.

But beyond the monstrous bodies inadvertently produced, the body politic concept has many heterogeneous layers to it, "thicknesses" to the body politic that may be stressed or de-stressed, depending on the context. There is, for instance, a medical-natural thickness to the body politic concept, in which the ideal body politic is "healthy" or "diseased" (as we find, in different ways, in Plato, Nicholas of Cusa, and Marsilius of Padua). The body politic also has a topological thickness, which deals with the network of relations between parts and wholes, between the "members" themselves of the body politic (again, occurring differently in Plato, Althusius, Hobbes and Spinoza). The body politic is also never quite rid of a theology that posits divine order and divine intervention as the hallmarks of "body" and "head," respectively (and thus the demonological aspects found in Paul, Augustine, and, later, in Bodin and even Hobbes). Not only are there great differences in any single historical period's ability to think the body politic, but the body politic is not simply a "political" or "theological" or "medical" concept. The body politic concept does not develop, it does not progress, it is defined as much by its internal tensions as it is by its repetition.

What, then, is the body politic concept? The body politic is a response to the challenge of thinking about political order (as a living, vital order). It is formally based on an analogy between the body natural and the body politic (through a narrative stressing unity, hierarchy, and vitalism). This formal relation is historically expressed in terms of political theology (and the questions of sovereignty and the "two natures"). And, despite this formal coherence, it is also a concept defined through its failure (that is, its internal tensions and corporeal variations). We have begun by talking about political order and have ended by talking about corporeal permutation, monstrosity, and headless corpses. Perhaps this concept, one that is so often assumed in political thought, is less familiar to us than we think.

*

Corruptible Bodies. Much of what is contained in the above principles is not, of course, new. A whole tradition of scholarship, including the work of Gierke, Kantorowicz, and Henri de Lubac has, in different ways, elaborated such characteristics concerning the body politic. Nevertheless, there is one aspect that has generally been under-explored, and that is the role that a "medical ontology" has played in articulating the shape of the body politic at different political and historical moments. This means, again, taking the literalness of the body politic analogy seriously – in terms of anatomy and the parsing and labelling of the body. While medicine does not determine the body politic concept, neither can the body politic as such be reduced to its medical content. However, what remains striking is the way in which the body politic is, on the one hand, always ascending beyond itself to a more ideal order, and, on the other hand, the way in which this ascension (or resurrection) is discussed in thoroughly corporeal, anatomical, and even vitalistic terms.

There is a great deal of ambiguity in the body politic concept, and nowhere is this more apparent than where the body politic fails to be a body politic, or where it fails to live up to its promises. A body politic that fails can only be understood as an aberrant or unhealthy body. And, at its extreme point, its very existence as a body contributes to an irremediable process of disease and decay that is at its core. Let us follow the analogy to its logical conclusion: in the same way that the body natural is open to disease, decomposition, and decay, so will the body politic be defined in relation to its own "disease," "decomposition," and "decay." Again, we can turn to Hobbes, who gives us a clear example of this logic:

> Though nothing can be immortall, which mortals make; yet, if men had the use of reason they pretend to, their Common-wealths might be secured, at least, from perishing by internall diseases. For by the nature of their Institution, they are designed to live, as long as Man-kind, or as the Lawes of Nature, or as Justice it selfe, which gives them life. Therefore when they come to be disolved, not by externall violence, but intestine disorder, the fault is not in men, as they are *Matter*; but as they are the *Makers*, and orderers of them... Amongst the *Infirmities* therefore of a Common-wealth, I will reckon in the first place, those that arise from an Imperfect Institution, and resemble the diseases of a naturall body, which proceed from a Defectuous Procreation.[25]

Hobbes, in whom we find a sort of culmination of the Platonic *polis* and the medieval *corpus mysticum*, carries the analogy to its logical (and bio-logical) conclusion. The body politic is not only constituted through natural law and the contract; it must also confront – and must continually confront – the immanent possibility of its dissolution. This polarization between constitution and dissolution in Hobbes is echoed in the Platonic body politic, which Socrates uses to make a direct comparison between disease and disorder. "When a person's unhealthy," Socrates notes, "it takes very little to upset him and make him ill; there may even be an internal cause for disorder. The same is true of an unhealthy society. It will fall into sickness and dissension at the slightest external provocation, when one party or the other calls in help from a neighboring oligarchy or democracy; while sometimes faction fights will start without any external stimulus at all."[26]

It is not just mortality that is a problem, but rather the processes of disease, decay, and decomposition that inhabit the very ontology of the body politic concept itself. Late medieval theology, concerned as it was with the problem of the "creature" and its dual nature (immortal soul and mortal flesh, incorruptible, more-than-human spirit and corruptible, animal body), also explored the connection between "corruptibility" and disease. In this connection, a fuzzy mixture of Aristotelian animism, Galenic humoral medicine, and the first stirrings of early modern anatomy all intersect to produce an inconsistent image of a body politic that is at once capable of an incorruptible health, and yet thoroughly determined by its corruptible lower half. For a philosopher-theologian such as Nicholas of Cusa, this implied that the body politic required an ongoing, special care: "And so like an expert doctor the emperor's concern should be to keep the body well so that the life-giving spirit can dwell in it properly because it is well-proportioned." Nicholas goes on to note that the watchful physician-sovereign should act once any imbalance of the "four temperaments" occurs, which can "produce various diseases in the body" such as "usury, fraud, deceit, theft, pillage," and "choleric wars, dissension or division."[27]

What, then, are the "diseases" of the body politic? Civil war, strife, rebellion, dissent, factionalism, mob rule – these massing, swarming, and ambivalent forms constitute the dissolution of the body politic. One of the lessons put forth here – and this is especially striking in the context of political theology – is that the greatest threat to the body politic comes from within; they are threats distinct from external invasion or war, threats that indelibly sweep up into a single motion medicine, theology, and politics. And, this pathology of the body politic was in place far before advance of the modern discourse of immunology and its tropes of boundary-management. Such formulations pose the possibility that the very structure of the body politic itself articulates a countermovement that is its own undoing.

Thus, to our previous principles, we can add another: *the body politic implies an anatomical framework that it is always attempting to supersede*. What is this anatomized, "medicalized" body politic? We have already delineated a number of its characteristics, and from our citations above we can highlight three of them. First, as we've seen, an analogical operation places the body natural in relation to the body politic, or, alternately, creates a fundamental premise concerning the relation between the body-as-natural and the body-as-political. For thinkers like Aquinas, this largely meant an infusion of Aristotelian naturalism into the theological concept of the *corpus mysticum*; for others, such as Nicholas of Cusa, this entailed direct appropriations of Galenic medical philosophy.

This analogy – between body natural and body politic – opens onto another analogy, that between the physician and the ruler, or between doctor and sovereign. At numerous points in Plato's dialogues, Socrates makes the comparison between physician and ruler, most often to show that the philosopher-king ought to act through a certain knowledge and technique (*technē*): just as the physician is skilled in the art of healing the natural body, so should the ruler be skilled at governing the body politic. This analogy finds its way into medieval theology, via the idea of a supernatural Messiah-healer, as well as via the secular variant of the ruler as the representative of Christ on earth. Healing, then, bears some essential relation to governing.

Finally, it is these analogies between body natural and body politic, physician and ruler, that facilitate an entire way of thinking about collective political existence in terms of a medical ontology. Recent work in science studies has done a great deal to elaborate the cultural politics of medicine, colonialism, and militarism in the 19th century.[28] Often such studies focus on the rise of germ theory and its attendant language of "invasion," xenophobia, and war.[29] But this is only part of the story. For, in its ancient and late-medieval variants, the body politic concept expresses itself through a dialectics of health and illness. Here, however, the lines between the supernatural and the natural, miracle and exception, theology and medicine, are not always clearly demarcated. For this reason alone, the concept is worth reflecting on. When references to pestilence or corruption arise in the writings of Aquinas, Dante, or Marsilius of Padua, it is not always clear when the reference is to an actual disease (interpreted in theological terms), or when the potential threats to theological and political order are being expressed in the eschatological language of disease, "corruptibility," and judgment.

Thus, while the body politic is, certainly, not exclusively a medical affair, this sort of medical ontology forms its central problematic. The anatomical view of the body politic is thus that beyond which the body politic must always move, but without which the body politic cannot be thought as such.

*

Only That Which Falls Can Rise Again. Every attempt to formulate the constitution of the body politic must also confront its dissolution – and this is inscribed and perhaps even prescribed within the body politic's structure itself. The body politic is constituted on its dissolution, the shaping of a collective, living body that always exists in relation to the corpse (*nekros*). We might, therefore, call the study of such phenomena a *necrology* of the body politic.[30] Its central problem is the correlation between the body natural and the body politic, but the correlation is never complete; the body politic never perfectly coincides with the body natural. The corpse – that which remains after life, after health, after the vital – this thing-that-remains becomes at once that which the body politic concept struggles against, and that which provides a promise of a more perfect, resurrected body. In a sense, the central problematic of the body politic is this anatomical and medical revenant, the body-that-remains. In other words, the primary concern of the body politic is neither a theology of spirit nor a physiology of organism, nor a physics of mechanism, but rather a necrology of the corpse.

We know that the concept of the body politic is predicated on a comparison with the body natural. And this opens the door to a pervasive, medical view of the body politic. We also know that one of the by-products of this analogy is that the body politic is also open to disease, decomposition, and decay. But is the thing we call the body politic actually, and not just figuratively, living? Is it not made up of the many bodies that form a single body? Is it not the actual life of the multitude of "members" that serves as the ground for the body politic analogy itself? At what point does the figurative collapse into the literal? What happens when the analogy of the body politic itself collapses, when it becomes pathological, or is subject to decomposition?

This is why it is worth thinking about the body politic concept alongside the historical and political occurrences of epidemics, plagues, and pestilences. Epidemic, plague, and pestilence – different terms, though for the moment they will be grouped together – provide us with instances in which the "diseases" of the body politic immediately fold onto the state of emergency occasioned by actual disease.[31]

In fact, this generalized medical ontology asks us to think of the body politic concept in the context of epidemic, plague, and pestilence, not because this has something to say about civil war or public health per se, but because it raises the philosophical issue of "the problem of multiplicities." This is the somewhat anomalous phrase Michel Foucault uses in his comments on epidemics and their relation to the body politic. The problem is always the management and regulation of multiplicities, and the problem is greater when the multiplicities in question are construed as *living* multiplicities. In his 1979 lectures at the Collège de France, Foucault outlines three epidemic diagrams that each correspond to a type of power. Leprosy in the Middle Ages, which is aligned with juridical sovereignty's power to divide and exclude bodies; plague in the early modern era, which is aligned with disciplinary power's ability to include, observe, and organize; and smallpox in the 17th century, which, for Foucault, is marked by a new type of power, an "apparatus of security" (*dispositif de sécurité*) whose main objective is to "let things be," to allow circulations and flows, and to calculate probabilities in an effort to effectively intervene.[32]

In each case, Foucault notes, the presence of epidemic disease puts forth a challenge that is fundamentally political: how to prevent the circulation of disease, and still permit the circulation of peoples and goods? Foucault formulates the problem: "I mean, of course, circulation in the very broad sense of movement, exchange, and contact, as a form of dispersion, and also as a form of distribution, the problem being: How should things circulate or not circulate?"[33] The main problem is not simply one of forbidding or allowing, but of regulating flows and circulations. Somehow the sovereign action of "shutting down" must be correlated with the security action of "letting things be." This leads Foucault to experiment with theorizing a new type of sovereign power, one that operates more through the regulation of circulation than through interdiction: "the sovereign will be someone who will have to exercise power at that point of connection where nature, in the sense of physical elements, interferes with nature in the sense of the nature of the human species, at that point of articulation where the milieu becomes the determining factor of nature."[34]

And it is perhaps for this reason that Foucault ultimately prefers the phrase "apparatus of security" to describe this combination of intervention and circulation:

> It seems to me that in the apparatus of security, as I have presented it, what is involved is precisely not taking either the point of view of what is prevented or the point of view of what is obligatory, but standing back sufficiently so that one can grasp the point at which things are taking place [*mais de prendre suffisamment de recul pour que l'on puisse saisir le point où les chose vont se produire*], whether or not they are desirable.[35]

If we again take up the over-arching question – of what happens when the figure of the body politic itself collapses – what is at stake is not just medicalization or public health, but this tension at the heart of political theology: the question of sovereignty and the question of the "two natures." The end of the body politic – both in terms of its aim, but also its more eschatological "end" – is its ability to effortlessly move between claims that are political and claims that are, in effect, medical. But when the body politic analogy collapses, as it must, it shores up a series of basic challenges for thinking about political order.

What threatens the body politic? It is not just figurative or literal disease, and neither is it the lack of distinction between them (which is in many ways the aim of the body politic). What threatens the body politic is something we can call, simply, "multiplicity." In what does this multiplicity consist? It is both constituted by and exists through its circulations and flows, by its passing-through, its passing-between, even its passing-beyond – movements that are, at least in the case of pestilence, plague, and epidemics, both the constitution and the dissolution of the body politic.[36] Multiplicity is, in these cases, not simply "against" the body politic in any sort of libratory sense.

A necrology of the body politic pertains not just to the moment when the body politic decomposes or dies, for it is in the very political-theological nature of the corpse to return, to be resurrected and reinvested with supernatural life. In the "problem of multiplicities" presented by plague, pestilence, and epidemic, multiplicity is never separate from, and always inculcated within, the problem of sovereignty. Perhaps we can say that multiplicity is the "disease" of the body politic. Or, alternately, it is multiplicity that "plagues" the body politic.

*

Necrologies. A necrology is, then, the study of the disease, decay, and decomposition of the body politic. But what is this *nekros* if not a certain decomposition of "life" and "order," a decomposition that is itself the dispersion or proliferation of the nexus between "life" and "order"? To simply position sovereignty against multiplicity is not enough to comprehend the corporeal permutations the body politic undergoes; sovereignty does not simply oppose multiplicity, nor does it exercise dominion over it in a recuperative fashion. How then to articulate the strange isomorphism between them? In the case of epidemic, plague, and pestilence, for instance, we are led to consider the massing and aggregate processes of decomposition and resurrection, of breaking-down and proliferating, of a passing-between and a passing-through.[37] These processes invite an examination not just of the pathologies of the body politic, but also of the *poetics* of the body politic. It is in the cultural expression of the living dead – and too often it is forgotten that the body politic is also a cultural concept – that we again discover this intersection between sovereignty and multiplicity.

Nowhere is the poetics of the body politic more effectively demonstrated than in Dante's *Inferno*, where we see stratifications of the living dead that are at once the product of divine punishment and, as such, are meticulously managed as massing or aggregate bodies. One of the most interesting examples of this is the sixth circle of Hell, where Dante and his guide Virgil come to the giant, fortress gates of the infernal City of Dis. Virgil must enlist divine intervention in order to pass through the gates, guarded by hordes of demons. Once Dante and Virgil enter, they see a city in ruins, an uneven landscape of burning, open graves:

And then we started moving toward the city [*terra*]
in the safety of the holy words pronounced.
We entered there, and with no opposition.
And I, so anxious to investigate
the state of souls locked up in such a fortress [*fortezza*],
once in the place, allowed my eyes to wander,
and saw, in all directions spreading out,
a countryside [*campagna*] of pain and ugly anguish.
As at Arles where the Rhône turns to stagnant waters
or as at Pola near Quarnero's Gulf
that closes Italy and bathes her confines,
the sepulchers make all the land uneven,
so they did here, strewn in all directions,
except the graves here served a crueler purpose:
for scattered everywhere among the tombs
were flames that kept them glowing far more hot
than any iron an artisan might use.
Each tomb had its lid loose, pushed to one side,
and from within came forth such fierce laments
that I was sure inside were tortured souls.
I asked, "Master, what kind of shades are these
lying down here, buried in the graves of stone,
speaking their presence in such dolorous sighs?"

And he replied: "There lie arch-heretics
of every sect, with all of their disciples;
more than you think are packed within these tombs."[38]

Again we have the ambiguous vitalism of the "shades" in Dante's underworld, as well as their massing and aggregate forms. But here the living dead are not simply a force of judgment or divine retribution; in fact, they are the opposite, that which is produced through sovereign power. And this sovereign power not only punishes but, more importantly, it orders the multiplicity of bodies according to their transgressions or threats.

In Dante's version of the "dead walking the earth," the living dead are explicitly included within the City of Dis; indeed, the living dead are the "citizens" of this city. As Virgil emphatically notes, the living dead are specifically politicized: they are the heretics, those who have spoken against the theological and political order, and, importantly, those who have done so from within that order.[39] The heretics, as living dead, are those that spread disorder from within the *polis* – through dissent or factionalism – and in this way Dante links the heretics to the inhabitants of the other circles of Lower Hell, including the "sowers of discord" (who are meticulously dismembered) and the "falsifiers" (who are ridden with plague and leprosy).

Nowhere else in the *Inferno* are we presented with such explicit analogies to the classical *polis*. The City of Dis is, of course, very far from the idealized *polis* in Plato's *Republic*, or the *civitas dei* described by Augustine. The City of Dis is not even a living, human city. Instead, what we have is a necropolis, a dead city populated by living graves, by the dead walking the earth. The City of Dis is, in this guise, an inverted *polis*, an inverted body politic.

In the *Inferno*, the living dead are not only a threat to political order, they are also organized and regulated by sovereign power. Sovereign power determines the living dead through an intervention into the natural workings of things, thereby managing the boundary between the natural and the supernatural. It does this not only to preserve the existing theological-political order, but also to identify a threat that originates from within the body politic.

Within this mortified body politic we witness two forms of power – a sovereign power that judges and punishes, but also a regulatory power that manages the flows and circulations of multiple bodies, their body parts and bodily fluids.[40] In this way, Dante's underworld is utterly contemporary, for it suggests to us that the body politic concept is always confronted with this twofold challenge – the necessity of establishing a sovereign power in conjunction with the necessity of regulating and managing multiplicities.

This is a remarkably persistent motif, and one found in the contemporary low-brow example of horror film. The peculiar sub-genre of the zombie film has, for many years, provided us with different cultural expressions of Dante's living dead. The American and Italian traditions are the most prominent examples in this regard. While early Hollywood thrillers such as *White Zombie* or *Revolt of the Zombies* placed Western doctors and heroes (or often the hero-doctor) within the context of voodoo and colonialism, zombie films after George Romero's landmark *Night of the Living Dead* (1968) place the living dead within a decidedly American, post-industrial context, self-reflexively stressing the "silent majority" through the use of political satire.

By contrast, the Italian tradition of zombie films displays parts of both the early and later American traditions. Though well-known horror directors have dabbled in the genre, it is Lucio Fulci who has explored (some would say exploited) the motif of the living dead in the most detail. Fulci's zombie films not only pick up on the idea that the colonial encounter is a medical encounter, but medical power is always linked to the supernatural – and sovereign – power to raise the dead.[41]

Critics of Fulci dismiss his work, noting that he basically made one film, over and over. And it is hard to deny such dismissals, for Fulci's films, such as the cult classic *Zombie* (1979; released in Italy as *Zombi 2*), *The Beyond* (1981), or the strangely uneventful *City of the Living Dead* (1980), repeatedly present an archetypal scene, one that visually encapsulates each of his films – that of the "dead walking the earth." The final scene in *Zombie*, for instance, depicts the living dead slowly descending on New York City as they cross Brooklyn Bridge (apparently the living dead come from Brooklyn...). Usually such scenes are moments of retribution, the living dead – themselves the product of a medical-sovereign power – taking vengeance upon their oppressors. Similar scenes are found in Romero's zombie films: *Dawn of the Dead* (1978), *Day of the Dead* (1985), and, more recently, *Land of the Dead* (2005), all contain key, climactic scenes of the living dead as a massing, contagious movement seeping through the fences, barricades, and bunkers that various human groups construct to manage them. The spaces through which the living dead move – houses, suburbs, malls, streets, city squares, military bases, and corporate towers – are porous to the miasmatic logic of the living dead.

There is, to be sure, a certain political romanticism in these modern variants of the living dead. Eventually, the multitude prevails through sheer persistence, and all symbols of hierarchy fall. All of this is not without a certain eschatological flavor as well, for, if the living dead are universal they are also the de-specified, a massing and ambivalent force of judgment.

In these archetypal scenes of the dead walking the earth, the living dead are driven by an ambiguous vitalism, massing and aggregate forms. They not only occupy the borderland between the living and the dead, but that between the classical philo-sophical binaries of the one and the many, the singular and the plural. Their massing and their aggregation is not only a matter of number, but also of movement (albeit a maddeningly slow, persistent movement...). The movement of such massing and aggregate forms is that of contagion and circulation, a passing-through, a passing-between, even, in an eschatological sense, a passing-beyond.

The body politic is not only a concept of political philosophy, it also involves a poetics, and both philosophy and poetics dovetail in this "necrological" point – the point at which consti-tution turns into dissolution, composition into decomposition. Viewed through the lens of Dante's *Inferno*, the body politic concept asks us to think the relationship between sovereignty and multiplicity, but as a necrological phenomenon rather than a vitalistic, heroic, or romantic relationship of liberation. The body politic is, by definition, that which withers and decays – like the cadaver. Something that decomposes and yet that is living.

*

Variations on Hell. Keeping with this theme of necrology, it is interesting to note how modern adaptions of Dante's *Inferno* attempt to show both the architecture of Hell and its many opportunities for decomposition and breakdown. Literary adaptations of the *Inferno* are too numerous to list here, though we might mention two noteworthy examples: LeRoi Jones' 1965

The System of Dante's Hell, which makes use of avant-garde literary techniques to recast Hell in terms of urban decay, with scenes worthy of Bosch or Bruegel; and Larry Niven and Jerry Pournelle's 1976 *Inferno*, which features science fiction writer Allen Carpentier instead of Dante, who dies at a science fiction convention and is taken on a tour of a high-tech, futuristic, theme-park version of Hell.

However it is in film adaptations that we see a stronger emphasis on the architectonics of Dante's *Inferno* as a whole, giving us a sense of Hell as a structural body politic. In 1911 the Italian silent film *L'Inferno* was screened, the first feature film to come out of Italy. It was directed by Francesco Bertolini, Giuseppe de Liguror, and Adolfo Padovan, and had taken over three years to produce. It contains, however, dark and magical scenes that have the power to fascinate even today. While the special effects do not, of course, compare to today's standards, the directors made extensive use of Gustav Doré's engravings of the *Inferno* in the composition of shots. Scenes such as the Circle of the Lustful make use of trick photography to give the sense of weightless, flowing bodies, suspended against the black sky by a torrential storm. *L'Inferno* makes use of the film frame in a powerful way, utilizing it to construct entire worlds with myriad things happening in each frame, and each frame connected to the next one by the passage of Dante and Virgil out of or into the frame of the film. The film frame not only gives us a view of each circle in a glance, but also serves as a kind of portal or gateway to the next circle, which we as viewers suture together in our minds.

This technique not only gives us bodies within the film – within the frame – it also gives us the assembled body of the film itself, the architecture of Hell as a whole, but one that we experience temporally, much like the reader of the *Inferno*. It is extended in Nobou Nakagawa's 1960 film *Jigoku* (*Hell*). Widely recognized as one of the first modern horror films to be made in postwar Japan, Nakagawa's film combines Eastern and Western notions of the underworld. The film is divided into two parts. The first part shows us the various desires, schemes, and deceitful dealings surrounding Shiro, a theology student at the University of Tokyo. Part melodrama and part crime thriller, the first part of the film depicts, in scene after scene, human beings preying on each other, each attempting to selfishly carry out their own nefarious plans. The first part of the film ends with a surreal, grotesque banquet that includes murder, suicide, debauchery, and several guests poisoned by bad fish. This gives way to the second part of *Jigoku*, in which we follow Shiro through the various levels of Hell. Nakagawa's use of saturated color and hyper-artificial effects gives these scenes a nightmarish quality. Amidst rivers of boiling blood and haunted forests, we see bodies dismembered and eaten by demon-like ogres. The more Shiro learns about the truth of human nature, the deeper he sinks into Hell. In an interesting moment of cultural hybridity, at the end of the film we see Shiro crucified to a Buddhist wheel of life, suggesting to us that the first part of the film corresponds to the second part, as Hell-on-Earth corresponds to Earth-in-Hell.

One could, certainly, continue to enumerate direct adaptations such as this. But we might take a different track, and think about how modern films have absorbed Dante's *Inferno* – with its architectonic spaces and passages between circles, and its evocation of strange terrains and stranger creature. For instance, Kiyoshi Kurosawa's 2001 mesmerizing film *Kairo (Pulse)* takes up the spirit of Dante's *Inferno* but incorporates modern technology into it as well. The film tracks a group of young friends as they become interested in video chat rooms on the Internet. Interestingly, Kurosawa films these scenes in a very particular way, often in darkened, silent rooms, with only the glow of the computer monitor. The video chat rooms are shown within the computer video frame as equally dark spaces, often with no one there. Kurosawa frames these scenes with the camera at a lightly lower position, completely still and motionless – akin to the films of Jasujiro Ozu. As the characters become more entranced by these seemingly empty rooms, strange suicides, agoraphobia, and depressive behavior ensue. Eventually we discover that the video chat rooms they are using are not connecting to other people, but to the realm of the dead. The video frames on the computer screen are portals to the underworld – and they are coming through.

Architectures of the dead, bleeding-through passages, gateways, portals. Numerous horror films show us portals to Hell in the most unlikely, most familiar places (a theme in films such as *The Sentinel* and *The Amityville Horror*). This is also a central motif in the 2011 experimental documentary *Devil's Gate*, by filmmaker Laura Kraning. A documentary without interviews or voice-overs, *Devil's Gate* is primarily composed of black-and-white shots of Devil's Gate Dam, located in Southern California. The dam was the site for a series of occult experiments in the 1940s by Jack Parsons, rocket engineer and co-founder of the Jet Propulsion Laboratory. Kraning's film focuses on the now-abandoned, desolate, haunting terrain of Devil's Gate, interspersed with excerpts from Parsons' journals. The imposing, abstract, geometric shapes of the dam are contrasted against the uneven, over-run, chaotic flow of water, weeds, and drifting mist. And yet the dam, product of human technological intervention, is also so embedded into the natural surroundings that it soon begins to look ancient, even primordial, as if it had been there all along. While adaptations of Dante's *Inferno* such as *L'Inferno* and *Jigoku* take us as viewers on a tour of Hell, other films, such as *Kairo* and *Devil's Gate* exist in the play of surfaces and secret, tenebrous portals. We become further removed from Hell, while it is, at the same time, more embedded into our living environments.

*

Argento's Inferno. A young woman living in New York opens an old, leather-bound book, written in Latin, its pages still unopened: *The Three Mothers*. It is by an architect named Varelli. In it, he tells of a coven of witches, each living in secret in three different cities – Rome, Freiburg, and New York – in houses designed by Varelli. He ominously refers to them only as *Mater Lachrymarum, Mater Suspiriorum,* and *Mater Tenebrarum* – Mother of Tears, Mother of Sighs, and Mother of Darkness. One of the architectural drawings in the book looks uncannily like the building in which she lives. Suspecting that she may be living in one the buildings designed by Varelli, she goes from her apartment down to the antiquarian bookstore next to her building, and inquires about the book she had purchased. The gaunt and curmudgeonly store owner lets loose only hints and clues, which deepen her suspicion further: "...the only mystery, is that our very lives are governed by dead people..." It is night. On the sidewalk outside, the young woman notices an iron grating just outside her building. It leads down into the cellar. Opening it, she walks cautiously down the stairs. The cellar is filled with debris – old furniture, rusted pipes, wooden crates, cobwebs. There is the trickling sound of water. It is coming from one of the pipes, forming a small, thin stream that runs along the furrowed ground like blood in the arteries. It flows further into the cellar, where there is a rough opening in the middle of the dirty and mottled concrete floor. It appears to be a puddle, but on closer inspection is an opening into an entire water-filled chamber below. Peering over to the opening, the woman's keys accidentally fall into the water, langorously descending into the water-filled chamber. Unable to reach it with her hands, she descends into the opening, swimming down to retrieve her key. She notices remnants of an earlier era – baroque chairs and candelabra, an ornate carpet, crystal glassware, an old fireplace, and dangling above it, barely held to the wall, a massive portrait, now faded, but bearing the Latin inscription *Mater Tenebrarum*.

There is a door that seems to open to still other chambers, equally submerged. Suddenly a flayed corpse floats by her, drifting upwards, as if reaching for the opening. In a panic, she swims up and climbs out of the opening. She frantically climbs out, quickly leaves the cellar, goes up the iron staircase into her building, and takes the elevator up to her apartment. Below, we see the cellar. Cracked beams collapse onto the opening, forming a kind of dilapidated, tenebrous, prismatic sculpture. An opera by Verdi begins playing.

*

Disastrous Life. "The disaster," writes Maurice Blanchot, "ruins everything, all the while leaving everything intact."[42] In our era of natural disasters, climate change, global pandemics, and the ongoing specter of bioterror, we are continually invited to think about the extinction of the human race in terms that are at once philosophical and at the same time in terms of the themes of which the horror genre is made. Given this context, it would seem that the body politic today is global and networked, viral and informatic, in the clouds, elemental, climatological. At its limit the body politic would perfectly overlap with the planet, resulting in the uncanny image of a living dead planet...

Crumbling cities, flooded cities, quarantined cities – the corporeal coherence of the *polis* seems to be constantly under attack at the very same moment attempts are made to re-fortify its boundaries and to re-articulate the conceptual apparatus for doing so. In the midst of these fissures and fragmentations, bare life is constantly rendered in its precariousness, a life that is always vulnerable, tenuous, happenstance, and therefore always an exceptional life. Nowhere is the precariousness of life rendered with such detail as in the medical and public health concerns surrounding "biodefense."[43] That the *bios* can be defended is itself noteworthy; but more relevant is the notion that the *bios* can be defended against the attacks of terrorism as well as the "attacks" of nature. In the case of bioterrorism, the two attacks become indissociable, culminating in a body politic that is both natural and artificial, threatened by the same form of life that constitutes it.[44]

Today, however, we no longer speak of the body politic; its terms are relegated to the obscure, dusty corners of historical and scholarly interest – they are dead metaphors. Yet, in spite of or because of this, what needs to be accounted for is the rather gothic longevity of the body politic concept. If today we no longer speak of a "body politic" this is not because the concept as such has ceased to exist. Perhaps it is because the issues that are raised by the body politic concept have never been so relevant as they are in contemporary philosophical discussions over the "state of exception," "biopolitics," and the "multitude" – in addition to the zombie-like proliferation of films, TV shows, and the like, all of which feature some variant of Dante's living dead in the City of Dis, the city that is a sephulcre, the *polis* that is, at the same time, a necropolis.

3. Meditations on the Gothic

Book of Beasts (Lautréamont's Maldoror). In 1868, a slim, anonymously published book entitled *Les Chants de Maldoror* appeared in Parisian bookshops. It contained only the first *Chant* or canto, and its purported author was the "Comte de Lautréamont" – much in line with the *fin-de-siècle* vogue for the gothic, the decadent, and a turn towards a literary, aesthetic aristocratism. In its posthumous life, the book would have a decisive impact on the counterculture, from Surrealism to Situationism. But at the time of its publication *Les Chants de Maldoror* (hereafter *Maldoror*) was completely ignored, even when Canto I was re-published in the anthology *Parfumes de l'Ame* a year later, and even when the full *Maldoror* appeared in book form.

It is not difficult to see why this book was largely ignored. It was neither prose nor poem, neither fiction nor non-fiction – it did not even fit into the popular genre of the *roman noir*, or the then-emerging genre of the prose poem. The following passage – from Canto II – is representative of many of the text's idiosyncrasies:

> There are times in life when verminous-scalped man trains his wild and staring gaze upon the green membranes of space, for ahead of him he seems to hear the ironic jeers of a phantom. He reels and bows his head: what he has heard is the voice of conscience. Then quick as a madman he rushes in amazement from the house, taking the first route available, and tears along the rugose plains of the countryside. But the yellow phantom does not lose sight of him and just as rapidly pursues. Sometimes on a stormy night while legions of winged squids (at a distance resembling crows) float above the clouds and scud stiffly toward the cities of the humans,

64

their mission to warn men to change their ways – the gloomy-eyed pebble perceives amid flashes of lightning two beings pass by, one behind the other, and, wiping away a furtive tear of compassion that trickles from its frozen eye, cries: "Certainly he deserves it; it's only justice." Having spoken thus it reverts to its timid pose and trembling nervously, continues to watch the manhunt and the vast lips of the vagina of darkness whence flow incessantly, like a river, immense shadowy spermatozoa that take flight into the dismal aether, the vast spread of their bat's wings obscuring the whole of nature and the lonely legions of squids – grown downcast viewing these ineffable and muffled fulgurations.[45]

Animals abound in *Maldoror*, but their functions vary, from the symbolic, to the scientific, to the absurd. The passage that opens Canto IV extends this litany of animalization across the spectrum of beings, from the human to the mineral, culminating in one of the text's many incantations against the human:

A man or a stone or a tree is about to begin this fourth canto. When the foot slithers on a frog one feels a sensation of disgust, but one's hand has barely to stroke the human body before the skin of the fingers cracks like flakes from a block of mica being smashed by hammer blows; and even as the heart of a shark an hour dead still palpitates on the deck with dogged vitality, so are we stirred to our very depths long after the contact. Such is the horror man inspires in his own neighbor! Perhaps I am mistaken to propose this, but perhaps too I am telling the truth. I know of, conceive, a sickness more terrible than the eyes swollen from long meditations upon the strange nature of man: but I am seeking it still [...] and have been unable to find it! I do not consider myself less intelligent than anyone else, and yet who would dare assert that I have succeeded in my investigations? What a lie would escape his lips! The ancient temple of Denderah lies an hour and a half away from the left bank of the Nile. Today countless phalanxes of wasps have taken possession of its gutters and cornices. They swarm round the columns like dense waves of black hair. Sole inhabitants of the cold porch, they guard entrance to antechambers as a hereditary right. I liken the humming of their metallic wings to the incessant clash of ice-floes flung against one another during the breaking-up of the polar seas. But if I ponder the conduct of him on whom providence has conferred this earth's throne, the three pinions of my grief give vent to a louder murmur![46]

Much of *Maldoror* displays this sense of a prodigious outpouring of word, sound, and image – pages on pages of thick, block text with dense, phantasmagoric creatures following one after the other. At some points the text addresses the reader directly, almost confrontationally; at other points the text digresses into long, quasi-scientific descriptions of flora and fauna; at still other points the text suddenly breaks into pulp horror or gothic romance. *Maldoror* breaks nearly every rule of poetics, though it does this less as avant-garde posturing and more because the text cannot help itself. There seems to be no end to what the text can do or is capable of – in a way, its length and division into six cantos seems almost arbitrary.

The one review that did appear upon the original publication of *Maldoror* expressed mostly a puzzled astonishment: "the hyperbolic bombast of the style, the savage strangeness, the desperate vigour of conception, the contrast of this impassioned language with the dullest lucubrations of our time, at first case the mind into a deep amazement."[47] The reviewer's reaction echoes subsequent mentions of *Maldoror* in literary criticism and literary histories. Such comments have always been brief and astonished, as if happening upon a strange but menacing beast. Antonin Artaud sums up the general attitude of 19th and early

20th-century criticism towards the likes of Lautréamont, Nerval, and Baudelaire: "they were afraid that their poetry might leap out of the books and turn reality upside down."[48] In fact, such comments on *Maldoror* are interesting for precisely this reason – they inadvertently treat the text as alive, the text as animal. For many readers, *Maldoror* not only confronted one in an abject, monstrous way, but the text itself seemed like an animal, a teratological anomaly composed of bits and pieces, a *corpus* left unfinished or untended. In contrast to the textuality of the animal so frequently found in literary representation, *Maldoror* seems to put forth the animality of the text – composed of multiple tendrils, leaping off the page, devouring the reader. In *The Romantic Agony*, published in the 1930s, literary critic Mario Praz includes only a few paragraphs on Lautréamont. But even in these few lines he echoes this tendency to treat *Maldoror* as an unnatural creature, referring to *Maldoror* as a "late but extreme case of cannibalistic Byronism."[49]

When *Maldoror* was "discovered" by the Surrealists, another shift occurred in the reception of the text: the animality of *Maldoror* suddenly gave way to an almost mystical quality. André Breton noted that *Maldoror* was "the expression of a revelation so complete it seems to exceed human potential." Philippe Soupault edited several editions of *Maldoror*, and Louis Aragon wrote the essay *Lautréamont et nous*. No doubt Breton, Soupault, and Aragon were taken by the often surprising juxtapositions in the text, the most famous of which is the phrase "beautiful as the chance meeting on a dissecting table of a sewing machine and an umbrella." But Breton's comments point to another aspect of *Maldoror*, one that extends the animality of the text, and that is its vigorous and persistent anti-humanism. While the Surrealists were unwavering critics of religion, they notoriously imported a whole host of mystical and occult themes into their works. Little surprise, then, that *Maldoror* – a text that would become part of the Surrealist canon – is frequently described in mystical terms: Breton evoked Lautréamont as "that dazzling figure of black light"; Artaud lauded *Maldoror* for its almost mystical, "perfect lucidity," an "orgy of the collective unconscious trespassing on individual consciousness"; René Daumal asserted that *Maldoror* was nothing less than a "holy war" on humanity.

These two views of *Maldoror* – as animality and as spirituality – often dovetail and become nearly indistinguishable from each other, resulting in what Gaston Bachelard referred to as "the bliss of metamorphosis." Much of this is borne out by modern literary scholarship on *Maldoror*. There is the question of authorship – the real person Isidore Ducasse, who uses the pen name Comte de Lautréamont, and about whom very little is known, except that he was born in Montevideo, Uruguay in 1846, and that in 1870 he died under mysterious circumstances in his Parisian hotel room. Literary detectives have noted the similarity between the name Lautréamont and *Latréaumont*, a gothic novel by Eugene Sue published in the 1830s. As for the title, *Maldoror* has often been compared to the French phrase *mal d'aurore* or "evil dawn," something that seems to be supported in one of the few surviving letters of Ducasse: "Let me explain my situation to you. I have sung of evil as did Misckiéwickz, Byron, Milton, Southey, A. de Musset, Baudelaire, etc."[50]

Further detective work has highlighted the many textual appropriations that find their way into *Maldoror*, from literary appropriations of Homer, the Bible, Shakespeare, Dante, Baudelaire, Maturin, to extended passages from textbooks on mathematics and the natural sciences – foremost among them Jean-Charles Chenu's *Encyclopédie d'histoire naturelle* (1850–61). All of the "facts" surrounding *Maldoror* seem to point to a text that, at all levels, attempts to unhumanize itself, divesting itself of authorship, authentic voice, and even significance. The text of *Maldoror* is predatory in its extensive borrowings, and, true to Praz's words, ultimately becomes an autophage, devouring itself in the process. As we will see, this tendency towards a self-abnegation at once corporeal and textual allows *Maldoror* to effectively collapse the distance separating the bestial and the spiritual.

*

Tooth and Claw, Flesh and Blood. Among the modern studies of *Maldoror*, there is a significant body of work that deals with the role of the various creatures in the text, be they fantastical beasts from the imagination, the more recognizable animals of the natural sciences, or the abstract idea of "animality" itself. But the critical work on *Maldoror* differs on how exactly to approach the topic. Some advocate an understanding of the animals in *Maldoror* through language and linguistic tropes. For instance, in his analysis of "animal similes" in *Maldoror*, Peter Nesselroth argues that the animals in the text must be understood within the context of the cultural representations of animals, a context that allows Lautréamont to play with the many strange comparisons between humans and animals (including the many insertions of scientific descriptions of animals). The result of such disruptions in the conventions of poetic language is that the reader "finds that Lautréamont is revealing to him a new mode of perception, a vision which is not restricted by the artificial limits imposed through culture, since the boundaries between the objective and subjective have vanished."[51]

Other approaches suggest that the strange and anomalous creatures of *Maldoror* should be understood in terms of dream, phantasm, and the archetypes of nightmares. This is what Alex de Jonge proposes, in his analysis of *Maldoror* as an extended "anatomy of a nightmare." Animals in *Maldoror* are often portrayed in off-kilter ways, either through an inversion of the natural order (talking spiders or frogs), or through exaggerations in scale (the glow-worm as big as a house). For de Jonge,

"Lautréamont distorts and destroys the essential matrices through which we decode reality. His distortions threaten our sense of space, of what is 'up' and what is 'down,' our ability to judge the relative size of images formed on the retina."[52] The particular types of animals that frequent the pages of *Maldoror* – insects, reptiles, amphibians – stand out in their radical difference from the human animal. "So foreign are they that they represent a devastating threat, a rich source of nightmare."[53]

Finally, there are those approaches that suggest we understand the innumerable animals, creatures, and monsters in *Maldoror* in relation to the concept of "nature" in the history of science, in which natural philosophy, logic and classification, and even theology go hand-in-hand. In an admirable account of animals in *Maldoror*, Alain Paris suggests that, in its excessive proliferation of life forms both real and fantastical, *Maldoror* borrows the model of the bestiary. For Paris, Lautréamont "is an explorer, an explorer of the human. An explorer of the inhuman, also, and particularly of the animal kingdom. From there the bestiary is born, like a diversion recorded in a log book."[54]

Though one can annotate each and every instance of this or that animal in the text, such tabulations will bring one no closer to the animality of *Maldoror*. In *Maldoror*, animals are neither exemplars of the natural world, nor are they allegorical stand-ins for human beings. In a text like *Maldoror* the message is clear: *animality is no way reducible to animals.*

The critical work to have comprehended this is Gaston Bachelard's 1939 study *Lautréamont*. In his analysis of the "animal life complex" in *Maldoror*, Bachelard suggests we understand animality on a phenomenological plane, as a "vigorous poetry of aggression."[55] For Bachelard this means understanding animals less as scientific species or cultural symbols, and more in terms of their affectivity. As he notes, "Lautréamont grasps animals not as forms but as direct functions – that is, their aggressive functions."[56] Animals never are, they always do – moving, growing, pouncing, and devouring. In this sense *Maldoror* is an inventory of affects: "A complete classification of animal phobias and philias would yield a sort of *affective animal kingdom* that would be interesting to compare with the *animal kingdom* described in the bestiaries of antiquity and the Middle Ages."[57]

One of Bachelard's most instructive analyses comes in his contrast between Lautréamont and La Fontaine. The latter, well known as the author of a number of beast fables, tends to portray humans in the guise of animals. The animals in La Fontaine's *Fables* only appear to be animals; underneath they are simply exemplars of human types and characters. For Lautréamont, nearly the reverse is true – humans, when they are present in the text, tend to look like animals, or are rapidly animalized in their actions. If La Fontaine is really interested in the human in the animal, then Lautréamont is interested in the animal in the human. Furthermore, in *Maldoror* humans don't just resemble animals, they frequently undergo metamorphosis and become animals as well. Bachelard stresses this active, dynamic, "aggressive" animality in *Maldoror*, in which animality is equivalent to function. This stands in contrast to La Fontaine, for whom animality is physiognomy, representation, and form. In the innumerable hybrids, teratologies, and metamorphoses that constitute *Maldoror*, Lautréamont introduces a concept of animality that is constantly producing life, life as presentation. By contrast, in the characterization and caricature of the human animals in the *Fables*, La Fontaine portrays life, life understood as representation. Whereas Lautréamont understands animality as an explosion of affects, La Fontaine understands animality as a set of behaviors. Bachelard summarizes these points, letting loose a hint of the romanticism that runs throughout his study: "La Fontaine has written of human psychology in the form of an animal fable, but Lautréamont has written an inhuman fable by reviving those brutal impulses that are still potent in men's hearts."[58]

Comparisons such as these allow Bachelard to draw out his major analytical contribution to the study of *Maldoror*, and to pinpoint more specifically the animality in and of the text. A catalog of the major appearances of animals and their actions reveals for Bachelard two major aspects that constitute the animality of *Maldoror*. There is the action of tearing, and its association with the physiology of the claw, the beak, the horn, and then there is the action of sucking, and its physiological association with the sucker, the fang, the mouth. For Bachelard these constitute the twin poles of *Maldoror*'s animality: "In fact I believe Lautréamontism is almost exclusively concerned with two themes: the claw and the sucker, which correspond to the twin attractions of flesh and blood."[59]

Furthermore, the actions of sucking and tearing are not exclusive to their corresponding, anatomical organs. The action of tearing (or sucking) may be passed laterally, from a claw to a tusk, a beak, or a stinger. Similarly, the object of tearing (or sucking) may also be transferred, from the flesh of amphibian skin to the smooth marble of a statue. This lateral transference is so fecund in *Maldoror* that it almost becomes arbitrary, obtaining an almost animistic propensity for the formation and defor-mation of forms. As Bachelard notes, in *Maldoror* "the beautiful can no longer be simply *reproduced*. First of all it must be *produced*. It borrows from life – from matter itself – elementary energies that are first *transformed*, then *transfigured*."[60]

In one scene described by Bachelard, the disembodied "spirit" of Maldoror is transformed, first into an eagle, then into an entire flock, and finally into a strange, phantom, "lost body" composed of a detached pair of albatross wings co-mingled with a fish tail, which then takes angry flight in defiance of "the Creator." For Bachelard, such moments reveal less about animals and more about the abstract process of animalization, signaling "a sort of vertigo of the animalizing faculty, which at this point will animalize anything. In its very inadequacy this instant biological synthesis shows clearly a *need to animalize* that is at the origins of imagination."[61] Thus, while there are numerous animals in *Maldoror*, for Bachelard they are largely subsumed within the affective physiology of tearing and sucking, claw and tooth, flesh and blood.

In *Maldoror* animality is in no way identical with animals per se, and yet the text is replete with animals, animals that come to us straight out of natural history books, but also out of the fantastical worlds of literature, the bestiary, and myth. This type of layering – animals in the text and animals as text – is something that can only be achieved in the "anti-generic" poetics of a text like *Maldoror*, with its many references, borrowings, appropriations, and modes of pastiche. A proposition, then: *animality is that point where the animals in the text and the text as animal converge.*[62] That point of convergence is, as Bachelard has already intimated, on the issue of form.

*

The Bliss of Metamorphosis. *Maldoror* is a text where the wild metamorphoses of creatures in the text are matched only by the equally wild metamorphosis of the text itself. So great is this animality of forms in *Maldoror* that production and destruction, generation and decay, forming and de-forming tend to overlap. In *Maldoror* "a living being has an *appetite for forms* at least as great as his *appetite for matter.*"[63] This emphasis not just on form but on life forms places Lautréamont in relation to Aristotle. While Aristotle's works in natural philosophy contain detailed descriptions of animals, it is in the treatise known as *De anima* that Aristotle talks about life in itself, apart from any particular manifestation. The question that guides Aristotle's inquiry has to do not just with understanding this or that life form but with understanding the life of every life form. For Aristotle, there must be something substantial to each and every form of life, such that we can say that a bird, a human, a tree, and an octopus are all alive. It is here that Aristotle proposes the term *psukhē* (often translated in English as "soul," but more accurately as "life-principle"). This soul or life-principle is, for Aristotle, directly connected to the form of any living being. As Aristotle notes, "the soul [*psukhē*] must be substance in the sense of being the form of a natural body, which potentially has life."[64] Furthermore, this principle of life forms is always form-ing, in the sense that it is an actualization of this potential for life: "The soul may therefore be defined as the first actuality of a natural body possessing life."[65] The capacity for form is, for a thinker like Aristotle, tantamount to the potential for life; there is no life without a form of life.

Against Aristotle, form in *Maldoror* is neither that which holds matter nor that which is abstractly shaped as an empty container. Form is not an end in itself, nor does form give way to the ontological priority of matter (even if this matter is viewed in terms of its vitalistic, emergent properties). Form does not lead to that which is well-formed, or in-formed. It is, to use Bachelard's terms, the dynamics of tearing and sucking, flesh and blood, claw and tooth; but these are themselves a manifestation of a more general animality, which is driven by an aggressive, generative, "appetite for forms." Instead, in *Maldoror* there is a sense in which everything is devoured by form, at the same time that form devours everything, including itself. In *Maldoror*, form is never formed, but instead devoured, metabolized, broken down, and reconstituted again in a new guise. The animality of *Maldoror* is, in a sense, the extension of Aristotelianism to its logical conclusion, in which the forming is also re-forming and de-forming as well. *Maldoror* is not exactly against Aristotelianism; if anything, it is Aristotelianism run amok, a feral Aristotelianism.

This "appetite for forms" has a teleology that is ostensibly spiritual. The appetite for forms is not arbitrary nor happenstance, in spite of its aggressive, instinctual connotations.

Bachelard suggests that the appetite for forms in *Maldoror* often passes through successive stages, culminating in an ecstatic, almost mystical state. The animality of *Maldoror* "would proceed through a world of living forms *executed* in well-defined bestiaries, then through a zone of *trial* forms that end finally in a more or less clear awareness of the almost anarchic freedom of spiritualization."[66] The comment is brief, and Bachelard does not follow it up. But the suggestion is an interesting one – that at the core of *Maldoror*'s animality is really a spirituality. The "spiritual anarchy" of *Maldoror* is a direct result of its aggressive, vitalistic animality of forms. At another point in his study, Bachelard briefly mentions an even more important phrase – "the bliss of metamorphosis" – to describe this intersection of animality and mysticism: "...there are passages that give clear evidence of the frenzy and especially of the *bliss* of metamorphosis... for Lautréamont metamorphosis is a means of executing an energetic act all at once."[67] Again, Bachelard does not elaborate or develop this mystical motif. But it is arguably central to an understanding of the animality of *Maldoror*. The "bliss of metamorphosis" not only describes an animality that is inseparable from a mystical tendency but it also attempts to conceive of form in a way that is at once the lowest and the highest, the bestial and the spiritual, the deformed and the informed.

Bachelard is not the only reader of *Maldoror* that has pointed to this spiritual aspect – and in particular, the defiant, anarchic spirituality of the text. Such a reading is implicitly a part of the Surrealist fascination with Lautréamont, and it forms an important part of Maurice Blanchot's study *Lautréamont and Sade*. More recently, it has been extended in Liliane Durand-Dessert's study, *La Guerre Sainte: Lautréamont et Isidore Ducasse*, where, contra existing interpretations, Durand-Dessert argues for a "religious war" at the heart of *Maldoror*: "This revolution in consciousness of which *Maldoror* is... the legible trace, is not in itself a new phenomenon, since it constitutes the foundation of all religions, and is something one finds is the basis of all initiatory traditions."[68]

In fact, we can draw out the implications of Bachelard's brief comments by re-casting *Maldoror* as a text on animality that is structured along the lines of a mystical itinerary. The text begins from a normative state of the human, structured along the division of life forms (human, animal, plant, mineral) which correspond to the division of life faculties (reason, motion, nutrition, change). We see all the exemplars of nineteenth-century European culture – the bourgeois family, the innocent youth, lovers and adventurers, men of science, and of course priests. But we also see criminals, the insane, grave-diggers, and the sick on their death-bed. In short, the life and world of humanity. In *Maldoror* this is the human world of science and religion, especially natural history and natural theology. Here, animality is always reduced to the animal, either in the form of religious iconography (e.g. sheep, goats, black dogs) or in terms of scientific rationality (e.g., the numerous appropriations of the *Encyclopédie d'histoire naturelle* found in *Maldoror*).

Into this world *Maldoror* depicts the invasion of animality, the invasion of the human by the unhuman. Sometimes this occurs via actual animals, chosen for their stark difference to the human (the various amphibians and reptile hybrids that populate the text), and at other times this occurs via animal assemblages (flocks, swarms, or packs of animals). At one point in Canto I this type of animality is depicted as a predatory, miasmatic force haunting both family and domestic space; this miasma turns into a pack of rabid dogs, which somehow telepathically connect to a frightened young boy in the safety of his bed, as he realizes his fate. In such scenes the human characters are confronted with something radically unhuman that they can only refer to as "evil" or "cruelty." In Canto II the discovery of a corpse in the Seine prompts a reflection on the arbitrariness of death; this directly correlates to an earlier section where the narrator imagines the corpse of God, composed of a multitude of fish and amphibians. Apprehension and dread predominate, as if the apparent order of the all-too-human world were suddenly thrown into abeyance. All human actions seem arbitrary, a pervasive sense of dread can suddenly come over the safest and most secure of situations.

Another stage occurs in which we see the animalization of the human – and the divine. Here, *Maldoror* moves beyond the confrontation of human and animal and moves into the terrain of hybridity, effected through Bachelard's two-fold activators of tearing and sucking. The relations of human–animal, animal–animal, and, importantly, animal–God are each played out through successive metamorphoses and transformations. Not only are there human–animal hybrids, we also see: a reincarnated, vampiric spider; a glow-worm's soliloquy on prostitution; a long elegy for a sleeping hermaphrodite-seer; a decapitated octopus rebelling against God; and a giant dung-beetle playing out its sorrowful, excremental, Sisyphean drama. Perhaps the most notorious example of this type of animality comes in Canto II, where, amidst a stormy shipwreck scene off a rocky shore, the narrator has a passionate sexual encounter with a giant shark.

The final stage of *Maldoror*'s mystical itinerary is the stage where the immediacy of animality leads to a pure openness of form in unceasing metamorphosis. The text departs from the animality in the text and moves out to the animality of the text itself; the scenes and events portrayed in the book – themselves appropriations from other sources – gradually give way to an almost purely arbitrary production of forms (an "anarchic spiritualization"). Vampiric fingernails grow over a few weeks, along with a craving for infant blood, there is a soliloquy by a hair found in a brothel bed, each of the body's organs turn into rodents or reptiles, God is transformed into a toad and then a giant hog, we see the world from the perspective of a python, a basilisk, and an oak tree, and mathematics becomes at once the most revered and most horrific of all things, the unhuman in its ultimate form.

Thus, insofar as *Maldoror* thinks animality through the lens of mysticism, we can discern a mystical itinerary, driven by "the bliss of metamorphosis," an animality of forms that has its telos in the dual negation of human and divine, man and God. In the final stages of this itinerary, the text moves from reproduction to production, from representation to presentation, signaling a shift from the animality in the text to the animality of the text. All of this proceeds from the premise that the animality of *Maldoror* is not reducible to animals. This in turn means a focus on the form-giving and form-generating process in life forms, taken to its extreme in the many cases of monstrous metamorphoses. Here animality is that form-generating principle of life (Aristotle's *psukhē*) that conditions the very possibility of form and forming, the very capacity for form. Philosophically speaking, such a notion implies a metaphysics of generosity, a commitment to a first principle of generation, fecundity, and affirmation – a first principle of a philosophy that, by definition, cannot be examined in philosophy. It is, perhaps, precisely for this reason that this type of animality takes on the tone of mysticism.

*

I Carry Around a Cadaver. *Maldoror* suggests to us a relationship between animality and spirituality, the "lowest" and "highest" orders, both of which are also decidedly non-human, even anti-human. And there is, undoubtedly, a strong anti-humanist thread that runs through *Maldoror*, evidenced not only by the violence done to nearly all human characters but also by the bestiary of animals, animal parts, and animal transformations. Human beings undergo monstrous transformations in *Maldoror*, while Lautréamont constantly rallies against the human in all its guises (including the human-made fantasy of an all-knowing God). In

Maldoror, "the bestiary of our dreams animates a life that returns to biological depths... All the functions can create symbols; all biological heresies can produce phantasms."[69]

The traditional view of animals in philosophy is often split: it tends either to reduce animals to their naturalistic substrate or elevate them into an abstract realm of flows and forces. Ironically, in the philosophy of animals, animals themselves disappear behind the mists of empirical observation, epistemo-logical classification, and the hermeneutic demand for myth, symbol, and psychological depth. Either animality is reducible to animals or animality is raised up to and includes human life; either animality excludes the human or it includes the human. In the former view – a lateral version of animality – all life forms are arrayed on a plane as part of the animal kingdom, each with differing characteristics. In the latter view – a vertical version of animality – all life forms are arranged in a hierarchy of capacities and functions. However, what both of these views have in common is a philosophical commitment to a *metaphysics of generosity* and prodigality, a vitalist ontology of fecund forms that constantly proliferate, generate, and change. The animality of animals is this commitment to the idea of a primordial, vitalist generosity of creation and form. Hence the philosophy of animals must presume something prior to the animal called "life," that is connected, in some basic way, to the generation and proliferation of forms that constitutes this traditionalist view of animality. This metaphysics of generosity is, in short, the a priori of animality.

At the crux of the bliss of metamorphosis and its mystical itinerary there is a philosophical commitment to a notion of life as generative, fecund, and proliferating of life forms. There is a metaphysics of generosity that determines and conditions the bliss of metamorphosis, and it is this vitalist metaphysics that also plays into the glorification of the human in terms of its creative capacity and romantic evocations of the "open imagination." In short, everything is generous, and it is generous for the benefit of the human.

If this is the case, then we can ask whether there is in *Maldoror* an animality that is not a vitalistic, generous bliss of metamorphosis, and instead its inverse: an animality that is the negation of life, of the withdrawal of form, of the liquidation and dissipation of form, of the emptying of all form – in short, an animality that likewise conceives of mysticism precisely as the dissipation of form. Is there an animality of absence, of distance, of opacity – a kind of tenebrous animality? If there is, it would mean looking to those moments in *Maldoror* when animality ceases simply to be immediate, while not being absent – moments when animality avails itself in its inaccessibility. Animality in *Maldoror* is not the continual proliferation of forms; animality constantly slips away, a single animal losing its form and becoming a swarm of animals, which in turn disaggregate and become indistinguishable from the elements and the atmosphere itself, all of this just as easily dissipated into the oblique and opaque *ideas* that inhabit the text of *Maldoror*.

Perhaps, then, there is less a mystical itinerary in *Maldoror* and more a mystical anomaly, an animal retrogression of mystical, spiritual heights, an interruption of divine beatitude through "tooth and claw," a mysticism that ends not with the fullness of the bliss of metamorphosis but with a different type of bliss, a gothic bliss of the loss of all form – especially the human form. Such a gothic bliss would require an ontology based not in affirmation and generosity, but instead in negation and dissipation – in short, it would require a negative theology. In this sense, *Maldoror* is less a vigorous bliss of metamorphosis, and more an incessant poetry of negation. The 6th-century mystic Dionysius the Areopagite articulates this contrast between affirmative (*cataphatic*) and negative (*apophatic*) forms of mysticism:

Now it seems to me that we should praise the denials quite

differently than we do the assertions. When we made assertions we began with the first things, moved down through intermediate terms until we reached the last things. But now as we climb from the last things up to the most primary we deny all things so that we may unhiddenly know that unknowing which itself is hidden from all those possessed of knowing amid beings, so that we may see above being that darkness concealed from all the light among beings.[70]

The negation of this type of mysticism is not a negation of privation or subtraction but instead a contradictory negation that is actually superlative, precisely because it forms the horizon of human knowledge. It is a negation that involves an erasure, an effacement, a denial (apo-) of rational discourse and thinking (phanai). Borrowing from the apophatic tradition of negation in mysticism, we might call this an "apophatic animality."

In *Maldoror*, apophatic animality has two aspects, both of which have to do with the negation of form. On the one hand there is *anamorphosis*, exemplified by the many chimeras, monsters, and hybrids that populate *Maldoror*.[71] A passage from Canto IV illustrates the dual process of the building up and breaking down of form that is part of the apophaticism of *Maldoror*:

I am filthy. Lice gnaw me. Swine, when they look at me, vomit. The scabs and sores of leprosy have scaled my skin, which is coated with yellowish pus. I know not river water nor the clouds' dew. From my nape, as from a dungheap, sprouts an enormous toadstool with unbelliferous peduncles. Seated on a shapeless chunk of furniture, I have not moved a limb for four centuries. My feet have taken root in the soil forming a sort of perennial vegetation – not yet quite plant-life though no longer flesh – as far as my belly, and filled with vile parasites. My heart, however, is still beating. But how could it beat if the decay and effluvia of my carcass (I dare not say body) did not abundantly feed it? In my left armpit a family of toads has taken up residence, and whenever one of them moves it tickles me. Take care lest one escape and come scratching with its mouth at the interior of your ear: it could next penetrate into your brain. In my right armpit there is a chameleon which endlessly chases the toads so as not to die of hunger: everyone has to live. But when one side completely foils the tricks of the other, they like nothing better than to make themselves at home and suck the dainty grease that covers my sides: I am used to it. A spiteful viper has devoured my prick and taken its place. This villain made a eunuch of me. Oh! If only I could have defended myself with my paralysed arms – but I rather think they have turned into logs. Be that as it may, it is vital to note that in them blood no longer pulses redly. Two small hedgehogs, that grow no more, have flung to a dog – which did not decline them – the contents of my testicles; inside the scrupulously scrubbed scrotal sac they lodged. My anus has been blocked by a crab. Encouraged by my inertia, it guards the entrance with its pincers and causes me considerable pain! Two jellyfish crossed the seas, at once enticed by a hope which did not prove mistaken. They closely inspected the two plump portions which comprise the human rump and, fastening on to these convex contours, so squashed them by constant pressure that the two lumps of flesh disappeared while the two monsters which issued from the kingdom of viscosity remained, alike in colour, form, and ferocity. Speak not of my spinal column, since it is a sword.[72]

In this non-narrative section we are given a monstrous version not only of the body natural but of the body politic as well. The body depicted is at once decaying and, one senses, about to crumble and fall apart – and yet it is also fixed, frozen, and petrified in its place. In anamorphosis one sees the breakdown of part–whole relationships, in favor of the play between part and part, but also between whole and whole. Anamorphosis can take place in space – as in the above citation – or it can take place in time, as in the final canto, where an archangel is turned into a giant edible crab, then into a fishtail with bird wings, and so forth. Anamorphosis functions on the axis of humanity/animality; its operator is that of decay and decomposition.

In addition to anamorphosis, there is also *amorphosis*, exemplified by the numerous instances of formlessness in *Maldoror*. Here, the animality of formlessness need not have to do with actual animals. Whereas anamorphosis is predominantly metamorphic, amorphosis is predominantly morphological, dealing with the limits of form and formlessness. An example is given in Canto V of *Maldoror*, which, interestingly, becomes a meditation on the poetics of the text itself:

Let not the reader lose his temper with me if my prose has not the felicity to please him. You maintain my ideas are at least singular. What you say, respectable man, is the truth, but a half-truth. And what an abundant source of errors and misapprehensions every half-truth is! Flights of starlings have a way of flying which is theirs alone and seems governed by uniform and regular tactics as a disciplined regiment would be, obeying a single leader's voice with precision. The starlings obey the voice of instinct, and their instinct leads them to bunch into the centre of the squad, while the speed of their flight bears them constantly beyond it; so that this multitude of birds thus united by a common tendency towards the same magnetic point, unceasingly coming and going, circulating and crisscrossing in all directions, forms a sort of highly agitated whirlpool whose whole mass, without following a fixed course seems to have a general wheeling movement round itself resulting from the particular circulatory motions appropriate to each of its parts, and whose centre, perpetually tending to expand but continually compressed, pushed back by the contrary stress of the surrounding lines bearing upon it, is constantly denser than any of these lines, which are themselves the denser the nearer they are to the centre. Despite this strange way of swirling, the starlings cleave through the ambient air at no less rare a speed and each second make precious, appreciable headway towards the end of their hardships and the goal of their pilgrimage. Likewise, reader, pay no attention to the bizarre way in which I sing each of these stanzas.[73]

Unlike other instances of animality in *Maldoror*, with their incessant biological admixtures and hybrids, here we have a sustained passage on a single phenomenon, that of swarming behavior that is at once tightly organized and yet formless and chaotic. It is also a passage that is itself borrowed from the *Encyclopédie d'histoire naturelle*, making the very act of reading the text ambiguous in its conflation of scientific description and figurative simile.[74] In amorphosis form is pushed to its limit, becoming either the absence of all form (the evacuation of all form) or absolute form (the devouring of all possible form). In *Maldoror*, these instances of formlessness can exist within a single body (as in the morphologies of the Maldoror character as a pack of dogs and then a miasma), or it can exist pervasively throughout multiple bodies (e.g. flocks of birds, a horde of rats, a swarm of flying squids). Amorphosis functions along the axis of humanity/divinity; its operator is that of dissipation and dissolution.

Maldoror is an anomalous text replete with animals of all kinds. It is also a text that is equally concerned with animality, an animality not reducible to animals, an assertion made in the text's frequent transgression of both naturalistic and narrative form. But the question is whether a text like *Maldoror* is about the production of forms or the loss of form, whether the text points to an animality that is driven by a vitalist generosity of life or by an apophatic dissipation of life.

Hence we have two variants on a theme, a theme concerning the intersection of animality and spirituality. On the one hand we have the bliss of metamorphosis. This relies on a philosophical premise, in which a metaphysics of vitalist generosity provides the backdrop for a fecund, proliferating creation of life forms – a bliss of metamorphosis that is ultimately recognized to be as spiritual as it is animal. With the bliss of metamorphosis, we have both a lateral animality and vertical humanity, the former by virtue of the many life forms presented in the text, which reach their highest pitch in a humanized capacity for *poiesis*. For the bliss of metamorphosis, animality is immediate and affirmative of life.

By contrast, we have presented another variation, which highlights the unavoidable anti-humanism that energetically drives *Maldoror*'s litany of assaults against both God and man. In this view, *Maldoror* is a text that rails against the human – and also against "life" (in so far as life is the privileged designation made by humans on behalf of other beings). While Lautréamont takes up the Aristotelian fascination with life forms, he is also positioned against Aristotle on the need for a life-principle and the metaphysical necessity of its ability to cause form to take shape. With Lautréamont, we move from the well-formed life (the life of, say, biological classification), through the form-ing life (the metaphysics of generosity, the bliss of metamorphosis), to a more suspect and shadowy region, a gothic mode where form and forming are inseparable from de-forming and unforming. If it is still "mystical," it is in this apophatic register, summarized in Alain Paris' study:

Lautréamont deplores the *human* form of conscience, which is duality and consciousness of this duality – that is to say, the consciousness of the separation of the self and the world, and of the self with itself... For Lautréamont, God frequently represents this alterity that both founds consciousness and the tearing of consciousness from itself... It is in this way that one must understand the hatred of God, invoked from the beginning of *Maldoror*, and not in the traditional sense of the problem of good and evil... There is a mysticism of hatred in Lautréamont. Hatred is a propaedeutic of the divine and that which is beyond the human.[75]

In Bachelard's reading, the animality of *Maldoror* lies in the "bliss of metamorphosis," a concept of animality that is a conjunction of the immediacy of life with a technics of form. In his evocations of the "open imagination," Bachelard therefore interprets *Maldoror* as a heroic type of poetry, an example of the modernist imperative to discover the new for its own sake. However, this tends to downplay the central importance of the gothic in *Maldoror*, both in its style and in its literary context. In this gothic mode, life exists only to the extent that it constantly ceases to exist; the prodigality of forms only exists in so far as they are decaying, decomposing, or disintegrating. In the gothic mode, animality is a form of life that grows by decaying, that is built in ruins, and that is prodigious in its nothingness. In short, *Maldoror* is less a *heroic* and more a *tragic* type of poetry.

Maldoror is a tragic type of poetry because it asserts that there is too much form in the world. This is because, as the stark, surreal scenes in the text illustrate, there is also too much life (and there is no form without life). *Maldoror* attempts an impossible task, which is to actively and continually un-form all form, above all that most tiring of forms, the human form. In spite of its many invectives against God, and in spite of its many absurdist descriptions of animals, the challenge posed by *Maldoror* is not a challenge against religion or science. The real challenge posed by *Maldoror* is this: *what is the most adequate form of the anti-human?* And yet *Maldoror* can only accomplish this via some form; hence its poetics of gothic misanthropy must take on the abandoned shell or the carcass of existing forms, both of literature and of life.

*

Against Literature, Against Life. Near the end of his study, Bachelard asks how a text such as *Maldoror* might impact not only literature or poetry but the entire field of poetics itself. It leads him to coin a somewhat cumbersome yet evocative term, "non-Lautréamontism":

> Ducasse's metamorphoses have had the advantage of un-anchoring a type of poetry submerged in the job of describing. In my opinion we must now take advantage of a life given over to the metamorphosing powers in order to move on to a sort of *non-Lautréamontism* that will spill out of *Maldoror* in all directions. I shall continue to use the term "non-Lautréamontism" while giving it the same function as that non-Euclidianism which can generalize Euclidean geometry.[76]

Bachelard's evocation of a non-Lautréamontism looks forward to the "non-philosophy" of François Laruelle, who also makes the comparison to non-Euclidian geometry. For Laruelle, non-philosophy is neither anti-philosophy nor meta-philosophy. It takes philosophy as its raw material, illuminating the "philo-sophical decision" that structures the separation of philosophy from theology, mathematics, or poetry, and that also internally distinguishes fundamental philosophy (metaphysics and ontology) from regional philosophy (the philosophy of religion, political philosophy, the philosophy of science). This philo-sophical decision is philosophy's necessary self-positing and the basis of its explanatory power. As Laruelle asserts, "philosophy is regulated in accordance with a principle higher than that of Reason: the *Principle of sufficient philosophy*. The latter expresses philosophy's absolute autonomy, its essence as *self-positing/donating/naming/deciding/grounding.*"[77] A non-philosophy would examine those aspects of philosophy that philosophy itself cannot examine, without becoming something else (a logic, a science, a poetics).

If we interpret Bachelard's proposal for a non-Lautréamontism or a non-literature in this way then the question would be whether *Maldoror* is a work of non-literature, in the sense that it complicates a poetics of balanced form and content, a literature of representation and hermeneutic depth. This returns us to our opening comments about animality in *Maldoror* – the animality in the text and the text as animality. *Maldoror* is non-literature because in every phrase it questions the "literary decision" that literature be at once apart from and yet engaged in that which it depicts. *Maldoror* takes aim at the human per se, but also at the cultural concept of the human as a literary creature, a form of life given over to reflection, representation, and the production of meaning.

But as Gilles Deleuze reminds us, literature is indelibly linked to life. However, this need not be in the usual sense, in which literature represents life, as form for matter. As Deleuze asserts, "[t]o write is certainly not to impose a form (of expression) on the matter of lived experience."[78] This is because literature not only transforms, but is transformed as well: "Literature rather moves in the direction of the ill-formed or the incomplete... It is a passage of Life that traverses both the livable and the lived."[79] If this is the case, if literature and life are connected not as form to matter but as mutually deforming and unforming activities, then what is the corollary for a "non-Lautréamontism" or a "non-literature"? It would seem that any non-Lautréamontism or non-literature immediately raises the possibility of a *non-life*, a life that cannot be lived, or, better yet, the "lived-without-life."[80]

Bachelard hints at this: "*Maldoror* can be taken as a pretext for understanding what a work would be if it were somehow to tear away from ordinary existence and welcome that other life which must be designated by a contradictory neologism as an *unlivable life*."[81] Like Deleuze, Bachelard also argues for a non-representational notion of literature, a notion of literature that is itself a manifestation of something immanent to both literature and life. But this also pulls both thinkers towards a metaphysics of generosity, a vitalist commitment to dynamic change and constant becoming.

Be that as it may, this relationship between literature and life is only given testament within the exclusive provenance of humanity. To whom is literature and its relation to life directed, if not to the specifically human life that is able to qualify both life and literature? This is one of the central challenges put forth by *Maldoror*. The strange proposition of a non-literature, a literature not intended for humans, would seem also to necessitate a non-life, or a life that is neither simply human life-experience nor that of the life sciences. *Maldoror* is in every way a text poised against the human, even in terms of its literary form.

Everything is possible in *Maldoror*, all hybrids are permitted, all forms only exist to be deformed and reformed. Teratology in fact becomes the norm, with its propensity for the aggressive, spontaneous creation of novel forms. In this sense *Maldoror* also poses a challenge to the principle of sufficient reason, a moral and theological principle that the world is well formed, and that the form of the world is necessary to the world. The animality of *Maldoror* puts forth what is really a philosophical challenge – it works through various textual assertions (appropriations, textual collage, unexpected juxtapositions), but these assertions are really negations, the negation of the bodies in the text and the auto-negation of the body of the text itself, as narrative coherence gives way to shards of surreal imagery and story fragments. *Maldoror* is, in a way, the most "gothic" of texts because it takes the gothic logic of decay and decomposition to its extreme point, where the text itself begins to crumble beneath its anti-human negations, its negations of all form – including literary form. As a book, *Maldoror* renders itself as a ruin.

*

Eaten Alive or Buried Alive. In his posthumously published study *Theory of Religion*, Georges Bataille discusses the relationship between animal continuity (the act of one animal eating another) and the life of the corpse (the process of becoming food for worms) – and the conflux between "meat" and "corpse." Just as the corpse becomes food for worms, so does meat emerge from the dead corporeality of the living being. But these are simply instances of a more generalized metamorphosis, of which the indistinction between eater and eaten, and the eaten and the dead, are its exemplars. This insight reveals an indelibly material aspect to what are ostensibly religious concerns, resulting in what Bataille terms an "ambiguous horror." This gothic horror is therefore tied, for Bataille, to the ambiguous horror of the eaten and the dead, meat and corpse.

But this ambiguous horror Bataille mentions is not simply the emotion of fear, the stimulus/response of fright, or even the existential dread of death – all of these imply an object of experience that threatens the subject, all the while maintaining a separation between subject and object. The ambiguous horror, in these senses of the term, is not only inescapably anthropocentric, but it is also invariably dialectical. For Bataille, however, horror is necessarily something unhuman. If it can be described in affective or even emotional terms, that is because it is, at its core, a fundamentally non-anthropomorphic affect – the affect of the unhuman. It is, really, a *religious horror*. Religious horror arises, for Bataille, from the "impoverishment" of religious anthropomorphism we cited earlier, encapsulated in what Bataille calls the desire for a "supreme being." The supreme being – Bataille's targets here are the monotheistic religions, though his claim also applies to pagan gods – is continuity recuperated into discontinuity, the God-made thing. On the one hand the supreme being allows for the Kantian concepts of causality, relation, and modality to be applied even to the supernatural domain, such that the supreme being has both "isolated individuality" and "creative power." In this attempt at having one's (theological) cake and (eucharistically) eating it too, there is the attempt to preserve the element of the divine as "indistinct" and "immanent existence."

The problem, for Bataille, is that in introducing the concept of the supreme being, one also attempts to comprehend continuity through the lens of discontinuity, in effect making the supreme being a being like other beings, along a sliding hierarchy of greater or lesser beings. "The objective personality of the supreme being situates it in the world next to other personal beings of the same nature... Men, animals, plants, heavenly bodies, meteors..."[82] The kind of equivalency that results is a relative equivalency between discrete, individuated things, greater or lesser, supreme or subordinate. But this generalized equivalency is not the same as the continuity (or intimacy, or immanence) of which Bataille speaks. For even though the concept of the supreme being is, for Bataille, universal, at the same time "the operation seems to have failed everywhere." At best the supreme being becomes a symbol, an icon, an image that, when examined directly, necessarily gives way to negative concepts (as in Anselm's famous definition of God, as that beyond which nothing greater can be conceived).

In a sense, then, religious horror is the implausibility or the impoverishment of the supreme being, at the same time that there remains something profoundly negative in the absence of the supreme being. Religious horror is the horror of religion – of its failure despite its success, of its all-too-humanity, of its claims for continuity in the language of discontinuity, of its confused confirmation and refusal of the Kantian antinomy between the world as it appears to us and the world in itself.

If for Bataille the "horror" that he discusses is really religious horror, what is it that makes this religious horror different from the other kinds of horror just mentioned (fear, fright, *Angst*)? One difference is that these existential-phenomenological definitions of horror rely on a basic metaphysical dichotomy of life and death, and the horror elicited in the passage between them. But there is a transformation that is neither that of life into death nor death into life, but a kind of hypostasis of persisting, subsisting, and abiding – the religious horror of passing time.

The tomb often comes to stand in as the artifactual symbol of this transformation, mediating as it does between the life above ground and the life below ground, the eaten and the dead. The tradition of supernatural horror provides us with non-philo-sophical presentations of these themes.[83] A case in point is the film *I Bury the Living* (1958), directed by Albert Band. Shot in the style of a film noir, the film centers on Robert, a successful but humble business man, who, through a chain of events, comes into ownership of a cemetery. As the reluctant owner of Immortal Hills cemetery, Robert eventually has his sights on the real estate value of the cemetery lots. In a wonderful scene that diagrammat-ically distills the entire film, we see Robert kneeling before a huge map of the cemetery, divided like a grid into individual plots. Those that are occupied have black pins on them, while those that are available (and available for pre-sale) have white pins on them. One day Robert's business partner decides to buy a cemetery plot for himself. That night, as Robert fills out the paperwork reserving the lot for his partner, he accidentally places a black pin on the lot. Days later, his business partner suddenly dies of a heart attack. As the film progresses it soon appears that Robert has the uncanny ability to literally plot deaths according to the cemetery grid – a gift he is horrified at, and of which he cannot seem to dispense. A grim reaper allegory, *I Bury the Living* places the living on a hovering, everyday grid of chance, a gift of death, and a map of mortality. Life becomes a waiting game, hovering with uncertainty in an uncomfortable proximity to open (and leasable) tombs.

For all its dread of an impending death, *I Bury the Living* retains the temporal boundary between life and death, with the tomb – vacant or occupied – as the mediator between them. However, something further happens in films such as *Premature Burial* (1962). Directed by Roger Corman and adapted from an Edgar Allen Poe story, the film centers on Guy, an aristocrat of an ancient and decaying lineage, who is obsessed with the fear of being buried alive. Despite the stern discipline of his sister and the romantic wooing of his fiancée, Guy's obsessive fear continues, derived in part from the death and internment of his father. It turns out that Guy's father was a cataleptic, often falling into death-like trances that could be mistaken for death. Convinced his father was buried alive, Guy fears that he too may succumb to the same fate. Determined not to do so, Guy constructs a sepulcher for himself that will permit him to escape from both coffin and tomb, should he be buried alive. In a strange mixture of genres, Guy's rather gothic plan for his "great escape" includes a coffin designed to open from the inside, a rigged gate and bell to signal for help, a rope ladder leading out through the roof, construction tools and dynamite, and, as a last resort, the ultimate escape – poison.

Eventually Guy does succumb to a cataleptic shock, mostly from his own, increasingly mad obsessions. He is believed dead, and plans are made for his funeral and entombment – not in the high-tech sepulcher but in an earthen grave. In a climactic, suffocating scene, Guy's cold, dead, motionless face, visible through a tiny window in the coffin, is juxtaposed to the desperate, whispering sound of his inner voice, which can only shout to deaf ears, "No! I'm not dead! – I'm alive!" This situation, which

Guy himself calls "this living death," opens onto a religious horror, a horror that derives not just from the fear of being buried alive, but, more importantly, from the comprehension of this hypostasis of living death, closed to the world outside and yet coursing through with a desperate vitalism.

Scenes like this are extended in Aldo Lado's 1971 film *The Short Night of Glass Dolls*. Combining elements of the *giallo* murder mystery with the supernatural tale, *The Short Night of Glass Dolls* is ostensibly a romance, but one in which love really is colder than death. The film's opening and closing sequences portray the paradoxical conjunction of thought and the corpse. We see a corpse in a sterile, cold setting – perhaps a morgue, a hospital, an anatomy theater. But as we watch the corpse, placed on a gurney, covered in plastic, shoved into a flat, horizontal locker, we gradually begin to hear its thoughts, presented in the film as a faint voice-over. *The corpse thinks*. And yet it is dead, its every thought on its own, contradictory state.

While there are examples of thinking or low-level rationalizing in some zombie films, what Lado does is focus on the metaphysics – the theology, even – of thought without a body. Here we have neither thought dissociated from the corpse and transcending it, nor do we have thought dying with the body, just as mortal as the body is mortal, indissociable from the mortality of the body. Rather, what Lado offers is thought tethered to the body, thought materially connected to the corpse. It is this thinking corpse that then proceeds to narrate, through a living dead anamnesis, the events that have led up to this point. What happens for the bulk of this strange flash-back is the *giallo* part of the story, involving a love affair, a missing person, a shadowy cult of the aged, and so on. The final scene returns us to this thinking corpse, which has now been removed from the gurney and is now in the middle of a medical school anatomy theater. As with *Premature Burial*, the living corpse can only shout to the void, "but I'm alive! – You can't do this!" But the dissection has already begun...

In light of this, we can describe Bataille's onto-theological problematic as the following: on the one hand, an immanent immersion in divine continuity, and on the other hand, a transcendental split between subject and object that guarantees the intelligibility of divine continuity. The former (divine continuity) can only be thought via the latter (subject-object split), but the latter by definition negates the former (the material dissolution of the subject-object split opening onto the material continuity of divinity). For Bataille, the only way out of this double-bind is by going headlong into it, and this means understanding religion in terms of horror. In this sense religious horror is a non-philosophical attempt to think of life in terms of negation, but a negation that is not negative. This life, at once a hypostatized materiality and yet an immanence of negation, opens onto what he variously calls continuity, immanence, or intimacy: "What is intimate, in the stronger sense, is what has the passion of an absence of individuality, the imperceptible sonority of a river, the empty limpidity of the sky: this is still a negative definition, from which the essential is missing."[84]

Bataille gives the name *divine* to this onto-theological problematic. The divine names not a supreme being or transcendent reality, but the necessarily implausible or impoverished character of the transcendent, when it comes to stand in for the discontinuity of continuity. But, for Bataille, this divine continuity must necessarily remain tragic, not "out there" and yet never comprehended: "This continuity, which for the animal could not be distinguished from anything else... offered man all the fascination of the sacred world, as against the poverty of the profane tool (of the discontinuous object)."[85] For Bataille this element of the divine is to be distinguished from animal continuity, even though it may derive from it: "The sense of the sacred obviously is not that of the animal lost in the mists of continuity where nothing is distinct... Moreover, the animal accepted the immanence that submerged it without apparent protest, whereas man feels a kind of impotent horror in the sense of the sacred. This horror is ambiguous..."[86]

The divine is, for Bataille, the irresolution of the material and spiritual. Divinity is not expressed in the heady drama of disembodied, ethereal spirits, and neither is it expressed through the back door transcendence of the ritual of the everyday. Instead, divinity for Bataille derives from the inaccessibility of the continuous entombment of the world, and humanity's *negative* awareness of this tangible yet inaccessible state.

*

Dreams of the Cephalophore. The decapitated body is, arguably, one of the most precise allegories of philosophy. The head, bearer of the brain and the seat of reason, is detached from a body that it can no longer govern. In the art of early Christianity, martyred saints were sometimes depicted miraculously carrying their own severed heads. These so-called cephalophores existed in the interzone between life and death, the material and the spiritual. Though their heads were separated from their bodies, they seemed to show another kind of awareness, the severed head held by the very body that offers it as a kind of sacrifice.[87]

In spite of their apparent isolation, beheaded heads are rarely alone. They are often put on display, and thus have the peculiar privilege of watching themselves being watched. They are also hidden away, and have the luxury of solitude, secrecy, hermeticism. There are really two types of beheaded heads (or post-heads?) – there is, first, the *expository head*, the head that proclaims, almost like a ventriloquist's dummy ("the sovereign law has acted" or "our band of raiders has visited this village" or simply "beware"). The expository head has a message (though not its own message), a message whose efficacy derives, in part, from the almost metaphysical presence of the head, and the equally metaphysical absence of the body.

By contrast, there is the *hermetic head*, the hidden head, the head for whom beheading is the occasion for despair and melancholy. Such heads are frequently found in horror film. Their most common manifestation is, interestingly, not as a head per se, but as a mask. Now, the mask and the head are not the same thing. What the mask adds to the head is not just a disguise, but an element of artifice. The mask itself is artifice, and when worn on one's head, the artificial is added to the natural, art to life. But the mask also suggests that, in fact, *all heads are artificial*. This is the case in genre horror, where we see masks and heads becoming confused with each other.

In *Halloween III* (1982), for instance, a popular Halloween mask mutates the head of the wearer into a goopy, bloody, mass. Here the mask overlaps with the head, sometimes resulting in a paradoxical decapitation of the mask, and the unmasking of the head. A variant of this comes from the Japanese art-horror film *Onibaba*. In the harrowing final scenes of the film, the mask cannot be pulled off the head, the two having become inextricably intertwined.

Films like these point back to literary examples, such as the Robert Chambers story "The Mask" (1895), in which an artist realizes that the best model for his sculpture is the human body itself, living, dead, or undead. The head is the portrait. The motif is explored at length in Edogawa Rampo's obsessive novel *The Blind Beast* (1931), where a reclusive, blind sculptor uses real bodies as his sculptures.

Perhaps the paradigmatic example of this hermetic, gothic fusion of head and mask is Edgar Allen Poe's tale "The Oval Portrait" (1842). The tale involves a painting session between a male artist and female sitter, alone in a rather gothic atelier. As the artist begins the portrait – itself an "oval" head – his attention is focused on the living sitter across from him. Gradually, however, he becomes more and more focused on the painting. At the end, the artist looks up – after an unspecified amount of time – and to his horror finds that the sitter has died, with only a decrepit, gaunt corpse remaining. While the tale is typically read as an allegory about art, mimesis, and representation, if taken literally (as all genre horror must be) it becomes a study of the real-time transformation of a head into a mask, to the point that the mask that eclipses the head, in fact becomes a death-mask.

Examples such as these involve a confusion of head and mask, so that really we should talk about a *head-mask*, in which all heads are masks (even death masks). But this can happen in several different ways. In Mario Bava's gothic film *Black Sunday* (*La maschera del demonio*, 1960), the melodramatic opening, which depicts the execution of a witch (played by Barbara Steele), uses the mask as a tool of execution – an iron devil mask, with sharp spikes inside, is forcefully hammered on to the head of the witch (who shouts curses at her executioners as the mask is hammered on to her head).

We are still in the domain of the mask as representation here, but just barely. There is still a minimal difference between mask and head, though the mask ultimately kills the head, the head engulfed by the mask.

A variant on this theme is found in Georges Franju's *Eyes Without a Face* (*Les yeux sans visage*, 1960). A desperate surgeon lures young women to his home, in order to graft their faces into the head of his young daughter, whose face has been irreparably scarred in a car crash. While she waits, the daughter is forced to wear an eerie, porcelain-like, white mask. Listless, melancholic, and increasingly mad, the daughter roams the house, the grounds, and the forest outside.

Without a face, the daughter also loses her head – all that remains is the mask, opaque, expressionless, and unhuman. In the final, haunting scene, she simply drifts off into the night forest, a body in search of its head.

There are also instances in which the head becomes a mask by virtue of its transformation into an object. In films like *The Brain That Wouldn't Die* (1962) and Stuart Gordon's cult film *Re-animator* (1985), genre horror overlaps with black humor and even slapstick, as heads are toppled, rolled, plugged in, and casually carried around. In *The Brain That Wouldn't Die* a husband saves his wife's head after a car crash; being a scientist he wires up her head while he seeks out a suitable body for re-heading. But the same old marital disputes continue, as she constantly berates him for his incompetence, her head effectively plugged into a generator. *Re-animator* goes further, with entire plotless scenes that are the result of a body carrying around its own head.

I leave the last word to Donald Cammell's harrowing film *Demon Seed* (1977). The film is mostly known for the scenes of sexual violence between the supercomputer Proteus and the wife of the creator of Proteus (played by Julie Christie). At one point Proteus, frustrated by the limitations of a disembodied, purely informational existence, attempts to construct a body for himself. These initial experiments – carried out in a basement workshop – are really attempts to construct material, physical prostheses, so that Proteus can act in the physical world.

In one scene, Proteus constructs a geometric "body" with almost infinitely recombinable parts, based on the dodeca-hedron. One of the nerdy lab assistants comes upon Proteus's unauthorized creation. After a brief conversation (and a failed attempt to convince him), Proteus kills the lab assistant, by actually beheading him with the dodecahedron. The pure geometry of the dodecahedron at once stands in contrast to the messy, flesh body, but at the moment of beheading, the dodeca-hedron also displaces the body. This is death-by-mathematics, the usurpation of the human by the strange matheme of the unhuman. Aside from probably being the only film to feature a beheading by a three-dimensional dodecahedron, the *Demon Seed* scene suggests something that is, at first, counterintuitive –

that beheading is always abstract.

*

Long Hair of Death. Hair is that part of the body that is also estranged from the body, that strange, almost inorganic matter that exudes from each of our pores. Sometimes hair is regarded aesthetically as a sign of beauty, while in other instances it is associated with strength and vitality (for instance, in the 15th century the *Malleus Maleficarum* prescribed the cutting of hair as one of the preliminary punishments for witches). A lock of hair given as a token of affection; hair as a relic of saints; hair bound in braids or unbound in fertility rituals; hair as a component of magical spells; hair ingratiated by extensions, hair refused by being shaved.

What I find most evocative about hair's almost mythical status is its ambivalent relation to death. Horror films excel at highlighting this ambivalence. For instance, take Antonio Margheriti's 1964 film *The Long Hair of Death* (*I lunghi capelli della morte*). Exemplary of Italian horror films during the 1960s, the film shows the influence of gothic horror classics such as Mario Bava's *Black Sunday*.[88] Apart from the requisite gothic sets (complete with tombs, castles, and thunderstorms), the film is also notable for its nearly incomprehensible plot, which involves the burning of a witch, a curse, a plague, and a string of female characters (the two main characters played by the inimitable Barbara Steele), all of whom are unwittingly carrying out a witch's curse.

In the opening scenes of the film, a woman in a feudal village is accused of witchcraft and sentenced to be burned at the stake. As she is taken to the site of her death, the woman becomes frenzied and panicky – her clothes are torn, her face is pallid, with dark eyes deeply set in her face, and her hair becomes wild and untamed, almost mimicking the flames surrounding her.

Following this, we are introduced to the woman's two daughters and a stranger named Mary, but they are all merely vehicles for the original curse. At the end of the film, the vengeful ghost appears to her accusers, back from the dead to perform an execution of her own. In the final moments of her revenge, she encases one of her accusers inside an effigy to be burned in commemoration of her death, an effigy that is now a sarcophagus, complete with brutish mask and long, black, straw hair. Though she plays several characters in the film, Barbara Steele's long, thick, jet-black hair becomes a leitmotif in the story. We as viewers cease to care about the intricacies of the plot and focus more on how the curse will inevitably be brought about, passing from one character to the next, through the woman's two daughters, through the character of Mary, and finally back to the witch herself, with the long black hair as the thread between them. The long hair of death stretches, like a curse, across generations and courses through different bodies.

Masaki Kobayashi's landmark 1964 film *Kwaidan* opens with the story "The Black Hair." The plot is simple – in ancient Kyoto, there was once a samurai who lived with his beloved wife. While the samurai would go out looking for work, his wife would weave at home. Tired of living in poverty, the samurai leaves his wife and marries into a wealthy family. His career rises, but he is unhappy. Eventually he decides to return to his wife. Upon returning, he finds the old house decrepit and overgrown, tall, lingering weeds sprouting everywhere. But there is a light on in one of the rooms. To his amazement, he finds that she is still there, sitting by the weaving wheel. Their reconciliation is tender and heartfelt. When he wakes the next morning, however, things are not as they seem. *Kwaidan* is based on the popular renditions of Japanese folktales by Lafcadio Hearn. The story "The Reconciliation," on which the film segment is based, describes what the samurai finds the next morning:

When he awoke, the daylight was streaming through the chinks of the sliding-shutters; and he found himself, to his utter amazement, lying upon the naked boards of the mouldering floor... Had he only dreamed a dream? No: she was there; – she slept... He bent above her, – and looked – and shrieked; – for the sleeper had no face!... Before him, wrapped in its grave-sheet only, lay the corpse of a woman, – a corpse so wasted that little remained save the bones, and the long black tangled hair.[89]

Kobayashi's film version stresses the stark contrast between body and hair, the decaying corpse set against the vibrant hues of the kimono and deep black hair. As the samurai recoils in horror, the black hair even seems to eerily move of its own accord. The hair is alive, the body dead – living hair, detached from the body, living perhaps *because* it is detached from the body. The samurai's face begins to turn pale and gray, his expressions are misshapen and monstrous, his own hair begins to turn white, eventually falling out in clumps – he becomes corpse-like himself.

Both films present us with hair – that strange, spidery, non-self – in some relation to death. In *The Long Hair of Death* that relation is only hinted at, but Steele's black hair becomes a silent symbol of the pending and inevitable return of the dead and the fulfillment of retribution – the persistence of hair as a marker of dread, beyond the life and death of the individuals that the hair "possesses." In *Kwaidan* the symbol is brought more into the foreground – hair is not only analogized to weaving and the spinning wheel, but it takes on strangely vitalistic properties of its own, out-growing and out-living its owner. Its power brings together death and beauty in a powerful concoction that physically overwhelms the samurai, draining all life from him and blanching his own locks with terror.

Horror films like these, in which a tomb is unearthed, a grave opened, a corpse suddenly brought into daylight – these films play on deeply-rooted myths concerning the mortality of the body. They also evoke more modern myths, the most popular of which is the notion that hair (along with fingernails and toenails) continues to grow after a person dies. How many scenes in horror films depict the corpse in this way, a shriveled and withered skeleton overflowing with tangled, dried-out hair? The uncanniness of this image – the body has withered but the hair has not – confuses the strict boundary between life and death, for how can the body, or a part of the body, continue to grow after death? What kind of body is it that continues to live on, after life? Hair – while part of the body – takes on a life of its own, even after death.[90] In death, hair becomes estranged from the body, an alien thing that seems to have neither purpose nor function.

Thankfully, the sobering effect of science has long since explained to us the myth of "death-hair." The corpse, no longer taking in fluids, becomes dehydrated. This process of water-loss in the skin (desiccation) causes the skin to shrivel and shrink, pulling the skin back over the bones. When this happens, the roots of the hair are revealed, giving the illusion of more hair than there is.

In these films hair is both unstable and contained, both formless and formed, almost sculpted by the almost embossed effect of their presentation. Hair is unmoored from its reliance on the body, becoming an unnatural thing, at once part of the body and estranged from it. Hair is always a problem. It always needs to be shaped and formed; it is, on its own, formless. Plato was grossed out by hair. In one dialogue he notes that of all the entities in the world there are those that are elevated and that have ideal forms (e.g. abstract notions such as justice or beauty) and then there are those lowly entities that are without ideal forms – "trivial and un-dignified objects" such as hair, mud, and dirt.[91] The hair that is estranged from the body – the hair of the corpse, seeming to ever-so-slowly grow and writhe on its own – this hair is neither living nor dead, neither a part of us as living subjects nor an inert object. Hair estranged from the body, from life, is really a non-life, perhaps akin to the ambivalent death-like vitality of other inorganic forms of life – choral, moss, fungi, or clouds.

*

Floating Abattoir. In all these variations, we see bodies decomposing, not just in the way that a corpse decomposes, but as living bodies, as living decompositions. The muscles and fibers of the body become a field of strange metamorphoses, the flesh grows at the same time that it is entombed, limbs become disarticulate and foreign, faces become masks, heads detach from bodies, hands hold our detached heads, and hair grows beyond the life of the corpse. Gothic anatomies whose various parts are all mutually estranged from each other in a kind of Aristotelian nightmare of parts and more parts. These are not coherent bodies, their structure obeys neither the strictures of anatomy nor the classification schemes of biological science. And yet, they are not simply irrational bodies, bodies opposed to the unity and coherence guaranteed by Enlightenment rationality. These gothic anatomies contain a logic of their own, one that centers on the various contradictions of the gothic – the fecund ruin, the living corpse, reason devouring itself, enclosures of vastness, the substance of shadow. The gothic fecundity of the body so vividly expressed in Lautréamont's *Maldoror* is given an equally stark form in the following parable, from Pascal's *Pensées*:

> Imagine a number of men in chains, all under sentence of death, some of whom are each day butchered in the sight of the others; those remaining see their own condition in that of their fellows, and looking at each other with grief and despair await their turn. This is the image of the human condition.[92]

Pascal's parable evokes an image of humanity as a kind of floating abattoir, the meat of the body subject to myriad, anonymous, inhuman forces that ensure its decomposition the moment we are born.

The image is given allegorical form in the way we as human beings relate to animals, especially those animals we produce and consume for our own uses. Georges Franju's 1949 documentary *The Blood of the Beasts* (*Le Sang des bêtes*) treads the fine line between realism and surrealism in his examination of a Parisian slaughterhouse. While its black-and-white footage and voice-over narration is straightforward and unaffected, the actual images themselves are anything but. From the harrowing images of the beginning of the process (workers mechanically killing horses or cattle as they come into the slaughterhouse), to the strange assembly-line manner in which their bodies are parsed inside (the uncanny rows of neatly flayed and cleaned legs, torsos, and heads), Franju's film takes the viewer through a range of affects, from shock, to disimulation, to a horrific fascination, and finally to an abjection that is, arguably, turned back on the body of the human viewer as the real endpoint of the process.

The Blood of the Beasts is, arguably, one of the earliest films to combine the genre of horror with that of the documentary. Contemporary documentaries, such as the 2012 film *Leviathan*, likewise combine novel approaches to documentary filmmaking (e.g. the use of lightweight, miniature digital cameras) with a stark and somber aesthetic reminiscent of the gothic tradition. An experiment in what the directors call "sensory ethnography," *Leviathan* uses high-definition, extreme close-up shots to give the viewer an affective, visceral sense of being aboard an industrial fishing boat in the North Atlantic. Images of various fish and other sea creatures are shot in such a way that they are at once grotesque and abstract, simply a wet, slime-ridden mass of entrails, chopped muscle, and cold, protruding eyes. Nearly every camera shot is from an impossible, non-human point of view – along a fishing line as it is submerged under water, the wailing gulls flying just above the surface; from up top a fishing crane as it raises a heavy, water-logged net filled with flailing, glistening sea forms; from within the bowels of the sorting containers on deck, the twitching creatures sliding to and fro as the boat itself sways on the tempestuous, night-time, ocean water. Gradually the human workers aboard the boat themselves become part of the visceral, abject seascape, the boat itself lost in the black abyss of an undulating, industrial night. "This," as Pascal says, "is the image of the human condition."

*

Molten Media. At the furthest limit of the gothic, the human becomes so estranged from itself that its very material existence is in question. The human vanishes into the animal, the beast, the creature; the creature vanishes into the anatomical happenstance of body parts; the body parts decompose and merge with other parts both organic and inorganic; and finally, matter itself vanishes into a materiality that is at once its fruition and its negation. At the furthest limit of the gothic, the human becomes fascinated by – obsessed by – its reduction into a black matter of oblivion.

Perhaps it is for this reason that so many horror films are as concerned with presenting shadows and darkness as they are with presenting actual people, things, and scenery. There is as much of an interest in decomposition as in composition, as much care put into the disintegration of bodies, spaces, and images as there is their narrative, filmic integration. We "see" both shadows and the figures that move in and out of them, but this "seeing" is of a different order, one registered on the level of paradoxes (the presence of a shadow that is itself nothing).

It would, no doubt, be going too far to suggest that every

horror film is preoccupied by these concerns. But at the same time, one can trace a lineage of these shadow-filled, "disintegrationist" horror films, from German Expressionist classics such as *The Cabinet of Dr. Caligari* to contemporary avant-garde films, such as Peter Tscherkassky's short *Outer Space*.[93] One of the classics in this regard is Mario Bava's 1960 film *Black Sunday* (*La maschera del demonio*). Shot in black-and-white, the film self-consciously references the gothic novel tradition, both in its themes (witchcraft and sorcery, a decaying aristocratic lineage, the resurrection of the dead) and in its settings (darkened castles, gloomy landscapes, cold cellars, and colder sarcophagi). While its narrative is fairly standard by the conventions of the gothic novel tradition, visually *Black Sunday* is unique among horror films. At a visual level it is nothing less than a sustained study of shadow and darkness in film, and as film. Numerous scenes depict one or more characters wandering through castle passageways lit only by a single candle, or often, by nothing at all. Bava simply lets the camera roll, filming "nothing" but the blackness of submerged shadow, at once flat and an infinite depth. The congruous spaces of the castle become separated from each other, almost as if the castle and the characters in it become lost in the material blackness of film itself.

This is the level at which contemporary films such as *Begotten* (1990) take place. Directed by E. Elias Merhige, *Begotten* makes use of innovative black-and-white film processing techniques to produce film that itself has the same gritty, dirty, material feel as the anonymous bodies, hair, limbs, soil, trees, mud, blood, semen, and other substances that populate the film's stark images. Though the film has a broad, mytho-poetic structure to it, it is less this that guides the sequence of images and more the interplay between the material in the film – flesh, mud, forest – and the material of film itself.

Existing somewhere between genre horror and performance art, *Begotten* is a ritual in cinematic time, enacted within a

primordial, mythical framework of origin and death, embodiment and dissolution, composition and decomposition. In
between these two points there is only convulsion. Bodies emerge
out of mud, limbs become solemnly entwined, distant figures
fade into dead forest trees, rows of sinewy, shadowy figures
crawl across a deserted horizon, hunched backs and arched
torsos merge with the stony tombs of cracked rock ravines, as a
granulated and shadowy sun sets beneath floating clouds of
black earth. The human bodies – if they can be said to be human
– disintegrate into their surroundings, just as the film images
themselves dissolve into abstract, abject patterns of saturated
black and white. There are no words, and breath is barely spoken.

The next step, presumably, would be to allow everything to
dissolve – human into non-human, body into environment,
image into emulsions of gelatin, crystal, and camphor. All that
would remain is to see film as film – in its temporal passing and
shifting, in its composition and decomposition. This is one of the
ideas at work in Stan Brakhage's experimental short *Delicacies of
Molten Horror Synapse* (1991). Though it is a later film for

Brakhage, it takes up his life-long interest in the abstraction of film as film, from his much-referenced *Mothlight* (1963) to the meticulously hand-painted abstractions of *The Dante Quartet* (1981-87). In *Delicacies* Brakhage uses abstraction to both comment on film – as film, as material – and to also allow film to aesthetically be what it is, nothing more than its material accumulation and disaccumulation. At just over eight minutes and without any sound, *Delicacies* consists of a sequence of hand-painted film frames in mostly dark colors. These are occasionally juxtaposed with sequences of black "empty" frames, or frames that appears to be scratched, scraped, or otherwise corroded. At points the entire mush of color and substance suddenly rise upwards in a weightless, ghostly levitation. At other points the abstract colors suddenly hold still in a kind of frenetic seizure. The colors frantically flow, then they freeze in a slow black strobe. The paint on film is by turns thick and opaque or thin and translucent. The unfolding of the film is this interplay of paint on film, chemical on chemical, material on material. From one perspective, *Delicacies* is a horror film, but an abstract horror film. It contains no story or plot, no narrative, no characters, no setting, and hence none of the decor of human drama. But it is also a film about composition and decomposition, building-up and breaking-down, and the inevitable disintegration of all that exists, the almost metaphysical corrosion that is at the core of being. It is even inaccurate to say that *Delicacies* is "about" these things. It is them.

4. Meditations on the Weird

Frozen Thought (Blackwood, Lovecraft). There are those moments when – alone, and before the breathable vista of the sea, a desert, a forest – there are those moments when "it" looks back at us, impersonally, impartially, indifferently. In Algernon Blackwood's story "The Willows," published in 1907, an unnamed narrator and his traveling companion – referred to only as "the Swede" – take a camping trip down the Danube River. At one point in the river, they enter a strange, eerie environment, covered everywhere by willows. It's nighttime, you're alone, you're in the middle of nowhere, and you're starting to get that strange, unsettling feeling that something just isn't right – you can see where this is going. The narrator, mesmerized by the slow, dancing sway of the willows in the night wind, begins to wonder if he isn't in the presence of something unnaturally alive. Strange dreams and half-visions follow. All of this leads the narrator to distrust his senses:

> I saw it through a veil that hung before my eyes like the gauze drop-curtain used at the back of a theatre – hazily a little. It was neither a human figure nor an animal. To me it gave the strange impression of being as large as several animals grouped together... moving slowly. The Swede, too, got a similar result, though expressing it differently, for he thought it was shaped and sized like a clump of willow bushes, rounded at the top, and moving all over upon the surface – "coiling upon itself like smoke," he said afterwards.[94]

When these vague and somehow alluring impressions become threatening, the unreliability of the senses turns into the incapacitation of the senses, rendering the narrator almost numb, and unable to physically react to his surroundings:

I gave one terrified glance, which just enabled me to see that the shadowy form was swinging towards us through the bushes, and then I collapsed backwards with a crash into the branches... I was conscious only of a sort of enveloping sensation of icy fear that plucked the nerves out of their fleshy covering, twisted them this way and that, and replaced them quivering.[95]

From here something further happens – or rather, nothing happens. There is no climactic and cathartic confrontation with a monster, nothing lurching or crawling inside the willows, no movement in or of the willows themselves, not even a man-in-a-monster-suit jumping out and giving his best cephalopod-like roar. There is nothing, that is, except thought. Indeed, Blackwood's story contains extended scenes that portray the absolute, icy stillness of everything, with the only movement being the very thoughts of the characters themselves. What are these thoughts? Quite simply, they are the thoughts of the unthinkable:

"Now listen," he said, "The only thing for us to do is to go on as though nothing had happened, follow our usual habits, go to bed, and so forth; pretend we feel nothing and notice nothing. It is a question wholly of the mind, and the less we think about them the better our chance of escape. Above all, don't *think*, for what you think happens!"[96]

Aside from the Swede's inadvertent inversion of self-help rhetoric, what is interesting about "The Willows" is the way in which the focus shifts from a horror out there to the concept of horror itself. This is the moment of frozen thought, the enigmatic stillness of everything except the furtive, lurking revelation of a limit.

These moments of frozen thought are not uncommon in the

genre of supernatural horror. Indeed, they become magnified in the early-20th century development of the weird tale. In H.P. Lovecraft's 1936 novel *At the Mountains of Madness* (first published in the pulp magazine *Astounding Stories*), an expedition to the Antarctic reveals the massive, black ruins of a "cyclopean city," whose very existence throws human archaeo-logical, geological, and biological knowledge into abeyance. In the depths of these darkly viscous and geometric ruins, the characters in the novel discover strange quasi-creatures that defy category and even description. At once formless and geometric, oozing with malefic intent and swarming with temporary eyes, these "Shoggoths" confront the explorers with their radically unhuman character:

> The shock of recognizing that monstrous slime and headlessness had frozen us into mute, motionless statues... It seemed aeons that we stood there, but actually it could not have been more than ten or fifteen seconds.[97]

In this frozen moment, the senses are rendered absurd, language begins to falter, and thought becomes strangely equivalent to silence:

> I might as well be frank – even if I cannot bear to be quite direct – in stating what we saw; though at the time we felt that it was not to be admitted even to each other. The words reaching the reader can never even suggest the awfulness of the sight itself. It crippled our consciousness so completely that I wonder we had the residual sense to dim our torches as planned, and to strike the right tunnel toward the dead city.[98]

In a last, desperate attempt to comprehend their situation, Lovecraft's characters resort to what is really an apophatic language, the language of negative theology:

We had expected, upon looking back, to see a terrible and incredibly moving entity if the mists were thin enough; but of that entity we had formed a clear idea. What we did see – for the mists were indeed all too malignly thinned – was something altogether different, and immeasurably more hideous and detestable. It was the utter, objective embodiment of the fantastic novelist's "thing that should not be."[99]

Lovecraft's stories abound with such revelations, expressed through the kind of melancholic, melodramatic, purple prose that has become a hallmark of the weird tale. At the same time, these revelations point to a minimalist limit that Lovecraft's characters can only negatively articulate: the beyond, the unnameable, the nameless thing, the thing on the doorstep, the lurker on the threshold, the whisperer in the darkness. In an interesting intertextual moment, the characters can only attempt to describe what they see by reflexively referring to the genre in which they are unknowingly embedded.

In so far as stories like these are part of the horror genre, they present horror less as a stimulus-response system, in which a threat elicits an emotional response of fear, and more as a kind of freezing of all affect, resulting in a combined state of dread and fascination – what theologian Rudolf Otto once called the *mysterium tremendum*. In stories like these, horror is a state of frozen thought, reason's dark cyclopean winter.

*

Logic of the Supernatural. In this state of frozen thought, the category of the "supernatural" plays a central role. However, the supernatural in this case is not the supernatural that is so often confirmed within the labyrinths of Scholastic theology. But neither is it the supernatural that is so frequently debunked by scientific rationality. In the horror genre the supernatural is duplicitous; it is the name for something that is indistinct and yet omnipresent, something that defies easy categorization and that is, nevertheless, inscribed by a kind of logic. That logic can be understood in several ways.

At one level, the supernatural can be understood as standing in an *either/or* relation to the natural. A character, inhabiting a world that he or she takes for granted as a world obeying the laws of nature, may be confronted with an exceptional something that cannot be inscribed within this normative, natural order. What results is a wavering, an indecision – either this exceptional something can be rationally explained, and what seemed exceptional is really just uncanny, or this exceptional something really is exceptional, and the existing natural and normative framework of reality must be re-examined, resulting in a non-rational acceptance of the marvelous. This wavering is what literary theorist Tzvetan Todorov has famously called "the fantastic."

At another level, the supernatural can be understood as existing immanently in relation to the natural. Here we do not have the mutual exclusivity of an ultimatum, not an either/or situation, but instead a *both/and* situation. If in the previous instance we basically have a theistic framework, here we have a pantheistic framework, in which the supernatural is revealed to co-exist with the natural. While this flattens the hierarchy between natural and supernatural, it also remains committed to a minimal distinction between them – while the natural may be taken "as is," the supernatural is never manifest in itself, and is thus not always available to thought or to the senses.

The question I'd like to pose is whether there is a third level, in which the supernatural actually bears little or no relation to the natural, in which what is experienced by a human subject has no correlate in the world or in thought. This is a sentiment frequently expressed in Lovecraft's stories, and more broadly in the supernatural horror tradition. Here the supernatural functions via a double negation that is not simply an affirmation

– a logic of *neither/nor*. Here the supernatural has no positive content; it neither stands in relation to the natural, nor is it an autonomous entity in itself.

Here the supernatural is a negative term. It displays an anti-empiricist tendency, in that it is not something that can be directly experienced or that is available to the senses. It also betrays an anti-idealist tendency, in that it is not something that can be inscribed within the ambit of thought – at least of human thought. And yet the supernatural persists, in its being unavailable to the senses, and inaccessible to thought.

In short, the supernatural is less about any relation to the natural, normative world, and more about the very impossibility of this relation, or indeed, of any correlation at all. And yet, as we've seen in our opening examples, this impossibility of the supernatural, this negative capacity, is at the same time manifest in the strange, unhuman catatonia of an impossible experience. The supernatural is another name for this enigmatic state of suspended animation, of frozen thought.

*

Neither Fear nor Thought. In a sense, then, the genre of supernatural horror is really about what it would mean to think this peculiar, frozen thought, the thought of the impossibility of thought. Understanding supernatural horror in this way requires that we read – or rather, mis-read – horror as a philosophical endeavor.

Here we need to pause and remind ourselves of the orientation of this book. Certainly, horror and philosophy at first glance seem to be diametrically opposed to each other. Philosophy is high-brow, the stuff of academia, professors, and abstract ideas. Horror is low-brow, the pulpy stuff of fan cultures, gore, and scare tactics. Philosophy, with its principle of sufficient reason, seems to say that there is an order to the world and a way of knowing it; horror, by contrast, seems to bypass rational thought altogether in favor of the affective extremism of fear and death. But there are a set of deeper, more interesting relationships between philosophy and horror. And we are, arguably, in a moment now where both philosophy and horror are discovering a common limit, which is that of the human and the non-human world of which they are, at the same time, a part (though arguably a negligible part).

Genre horror is, generally speaking, inscribed within two philosophical paradigms. The first is a Kantian paradigm, one that involves the balanced interplay between the senses, the understanding, and reason. In Kant's normative model, while aesthetic experience is made possible by sensory apprehension, it is ultimately qualified by the understanding and reason. Even those anomalous moments in which the senses threaten to overwhelm reason, are, in the end, recuperated within reason's comprehension of its being overwhelmed. For instance, Kant's well-known distinction between the beautiful and the sublime rests on the problem of form and formlessness:

> The beautiful in nature is a question of the form of the object, and this consists in limitation, whereas the sublime is to be found in an object even devoid of form, so far as it immediately involves, or else by its presence provokes, a representation of *limitlessness*, yet with a super-added thought of its totality.[100]

We need not go over the exhaustive list of interpretations of the Kantian sublime. Suffice it to say that in the sublime there is an ambivalence at work, a tension between a supposedly well-formed subject and a formless, boundless object – a non-object, really. In short, Kant describes an aesthetic relation to something that is, strangely, nothing. The consolation prize for us as subjects is that while we cannot fully comprehend this non-object, this nothing, we can, at the very least, comprehend this incomprehension – we can think the failure of thought.

So fundamental is this ambivalence to Kant's philosophical project that he goes on to characterize the sublime as a "negative pleasure," in language that seems not that far removed from Blackwood or Lovecraft:

> ...the feeling of the sublime is a pleasure that only arises indirectly, being brought about by a feeling of a momentary check to the vital forces followed at once by a discharge all the more powerful... the delight in the sublime does not so much involve positive pleasure as admiration or respect, i.e. merits the name of a negative pleasure.[101]

While the experience of the beautiful has a purpose, in that it establishes a certain harmony within the imagination, the sublime for Kant seems to have no purpose except its own undoing, its own disintegration. In Kant's words, the sublime "does violence to the imagination; and yet it is judged to be only the more sublime."

But for Kant the real pay-off of the sublime lies not in its excess or its capacity to overwhelm the subject, but in this final, recuperative move in which the very failure of the aesthetic is circumscribed by thought, and the subject able to minimally comprehend its own dissolution. What Kant has notoriously called "supersensible reason" effectively comes in to save the day. As he notes, "[t]he sublime is that, the mere capability of thinking which evidences a faculty of mind transcending every standard of sense."[102]

So then, what exactly is the Kantian paradigm of horror? Horror is, as the story goes, a certain imbalance within this set of relations. Horror is the always-potential threat of the senses being overwhelmed, of something being sensed that is in excess of the sorting mechanism of the understanding, and the synthetic function of reason. Horror is a case of the sublime – even if, in Kant's version of the story, this excess, this being overwhelmed, is ultimately recuperated by reflexive, supersensible reason, and thereby domesticated within the confines of an internalized self correlating to an external world.

To be more direct, we might say that the Kantian paradigm of horror understands horror in terms of the emotion of fear. Horror is equivalent to fear. It goes without saying that today this has come to be the defining element of genre horror in the popular mindset. Film-makers, authors, and scholars repeat it almost as a mantra: horror is fear.

This fear specific to horror encompasses a number of variations. One of them is the gothic distinction between "terror" and "horror," famously encapsulated in Ann Radcliffe's 1826 article, "On the Supernatural in Poetry." The distinction between terror and horror is at once a temporal and a spatial distinction. In terror, there is the obscure apprehension of something malefic that is about to happen, whereas with horror there is a revulsion towards what has just happened.

This equation between horror and fear also encompasses the more existential distinction between "fear" and "dread," detailed in Kierkegaard's 1844 philosophical fiction, *The Concept of Dread*. In his famous analogy, when standing on a cliff before an abyss, we not only feel the fear of possibly falling to our death, but we also entertain the impulse to willingly dive into the abyss, as into something utterly unknown. At such moments one registers the distinction between that which has a distinct object of fear, and dread, or the "unfocused fear" before the abyss of uncertainty. As Kierkegaard notes, "dread is the vertigo of freedom."

While both of these distinctions are interesting in themselves, in both the gothic and existential variants, horror continues to be understood as being equivalent to fear generally. The result is that this ends up defining horror within a Kantian paradigm, in which fear is situated in the relation between an experiencing, affected subject, and an affecting object that is the source of fear for the subject.

However, Lovecraft provides us with a different story. In his 1927 essay *Supernatural Horror in Literature*, Lovecraft provides a list of qualities that he deems proper to supernatural horror:

> The true weird tale has something more than secret murder, bloody bones, or a sheeted skeleton form clanking chains according to rule. A certain atmosphere of breathless and unexplainable dread of outer, unknown forces must be present; and there must be a hint, expressed with a seriousness and portentousness becoming its subject, of that most terrible conception of the human brain – a malign and particular suspension or defeat of those fixed laws of Nature which are our only safeguard against the assaults of chaos and the daemons of unplumbed space.[103]

Lovecraft was a staunch atheist, and yet his descriptions here and elsewhere in the essay also betray a sense of wonder, of the mysterious – even, dare we say, of a religious quality – but a religiousness in the absence of any God whatsoever.

Lovecraft's most concise definition comes in the opening pages of the essay. As he notes, "[t]he oldest and strongest emotion of mankind is fear, and oldest and strongest kind of fear is fear of the unknown."[104] Let us state Lovecraft's formula plainly: horror is the fear of the unknown.

Now, on the surface, it appears that Lovecraft is simply reiterating the Kantian paradigm of horror, where horror is equivalent to fear. But a more careful reading reveals something different, and that is a shift in this very phrase, "fear of the unknown." I would like to suggest that Lovecraft's insight is to have shifted the emphasis, from the "fear" part of that phrase, to the "unknown" part:

The one test of the really weird is simply this – whether or not there be excited in the reader a profound sense of dread, and of contact with unknown spheres and powers; a subtle attitude of awed listening, as if for the beating of black wings or the scratching of outside shapes and entities on the known universe's utmost rim.[105]

One of the ideas that Lovecraft returns to again and again is this notion of the unknown, in which horror is less defined by emotion, and more by thought – or, to be more precise, the limit of thought. And this is where I think Lovecraft departs from Kant. For, while both are concerned with the limits of thought, Lovecraft does not maintain the same faith in "supersensible reason" that we see in Kant. Perhaps we can paraphrase their differences by saying that, while Kant is concerned with the limit *of* thought, Lovecraft is concerned with limit *as* thought. The horror is not that there is a limit to thought; that is simply a regulatory gesture, a relative problem, a case of boundary-management. Rather, the horror is that thought – all thought, since for Lovecraft everything is absolute – all thought is paradoxically constituted as limit, a strange but perhaps enchanting abyss at the core of thought itself.

For writers like Lovecraft, the thought that comes to define horror is a concept with no content, an unknown in which it is thought itself that falters. For example, in Lovecraft's 1936 story "The Shadow Out of Time," the narrator, following a sudden collapse and comatose state, describes being beset by "vague and frightful speculations." Strange dream images form in his mind, of "a ghastly, fungoid pallor," and "great shapeless suggestions of shadow." Eventually the narrator is forced to confront the possibility that his dreams are not just dreams. A strange lucidity follows:

I looked for an instant, then almost collapsed. Clenching my teeth, however, I kept silence. I sank wholly to the floor and put a hand to my forehead amidst the engulfing blackness. What I dreaded and expected was there. Either I was dreaming, or time and space had become a mockery.[106]

Here horror is not the fullness of feeling, but the emptiness of thought. Horror is not the overflowing, psychological continuum of experience, but the vacuity of any correlation between subject and object, between self and world.

*

Neither Life nor Death. I mentioned that horror is inscribed by two dominant paradigms. In addition to the Kantian paradigm (where horror is equivalent to fear), there is a second paradigm, a Heideggerian one, in which fear is qualified in its relation to death. Again, this is not the place to provide a summary of Heidegger's *Being and Time*, nor to elaborate on the various esoteric schools of Heideggerian, hermeneutic, and phenomenological thought that flow from that work. Instead, we can simply highlight the role that death plays in Heidegger's thought, using that to characterize another aspect of genre horror.

We saw that in the Kantian paradigm, horror was broadly equivalent to an emotional state, that of fear. But this is an incomplete picture. Horror is not simply equal to fear, for fear is always prepositional, always "fear of." Horror is fear, yes, but fear of what? Fear of the loss of individuality, fear of the loss of individuation, fear of the loss of control, fear of fate, accident, or superstition, and above all, fear of death – especially one's own death. Again, as the story goes, horror is not just about fear, but is ultimately about the fear of death.

But for Heidegger, not all death is equal. There is "perishing," or the physical, biological death of the living being, and then there is "demise," or the set of rituals and practices surrounding death that are part of human cultures. Death (with a capital "D") grounds both perishing and demise, precisely because it is never present to us in itself, and cannot be the concrete object of any experience. As human beings, thrown into the world, Being is always being-there (*Da-sein*); hence what we experience is only this partial being-in-the-world, even though we may speculate on Being in general, or the Being of all beings. But the dream of a complete, unified, and coherent picture of the world constantly eludes us. As beings-in-the-world, we are also beings-in-time, inscribed within the flux and flow of temporality, of what Aristotle termed coming-to-be and passing-away. From one perspective, Death seems to be the promise of this completion and unity, but of course one never experiences one's own Death. Though we may witness the perishing of another living being, and we may feel for the demise of another, for each subject Death remains an enigma, at once negation and fulfillment, the abyss of non-existence and the promise of the unity of our being.

So the human being, thrown into the world, inscribed within temporal incompletion, struggles to comprehend the world and its being – Dasein struggles to comprehend something that is by definition incomplete. For Heidegger, Death is this incompletion. In his formulation, Death is one's "ownmost" (individuated towards the human subject), it is "non-relational" (it cannot be shared), and it is "not to be outstripped" (it is both inevitable and also indeterminate). With Heidegger, as with Kant, there is a consolation prize for the failure of the human to fully comprehend the world. We may not experience Death directly, and we may not be able to fully think Death, but we can think this failure. Death shifts from being thought of as standing in contrast to life (either as opposed to life, as negating life, or as sequentially signaling the end of life), to being immanent in life itself. For the being that has realized this (and this of course means human beings), Death actually opens onto the "call of conscience," care, and the concern with authenticity. Heidegger famously calls this attitude "Being-towards-Death."

It goes without saying that the horror genre is replete with instances of Death in Heidegger's sense. But it often cloaks these in the guise of perishing or demise. Thus, behind all the explicit focus in the horror genres on fear, fright, and terror, there is the implicit and more general concern with death. In short, in the Heideggerian paradigm, horror is defined not by fear but by death, in so far as horror is centrally concerned with the problem of Being, beings, and the lives of beings. And, in this Heideggerian paradigm, there is a therapeutic function to philosophy as well. Death reveals the possibility of specifically human life as authentic and as existentially unique. Death makes possible the explicitly human concerns of salvation, redemption, remembrance. Indeed, it would not be going too far to say that there is a humanism – often of the most conservative type – that runs through the horror genre. This is the truth of horror – Life conditioned by Death, human beings conditioned by Being in general, our ontical "being-in-the-world" conditioned by an anxious Being-towards-Death. The truth of horror lies in this therapeutic function of the value of human finitude in its factical being, its singularity, its being-there (*da-sein*).

Here again Lovecraft offers a different perspective. For Lovecraft, horror is defined precisely by its having no truth to tell vis-à-vis humanity – except this non-truth. For Lovecraft, one does not leave a tale of supernatural horror feeling better, or, for that matter, feeling anything at all. There is no truth to horror, in the sense that one ultimately discovers a state of being-there that is the exclusive provenance of human beings and their capacity to seek out authentic lives. If anything, supernatural horror is, for Lovecraft, defined by an anti-humanism, one that questions the entire ontic and ontological apparatus in which we as human beings grant ourselves privileged points of access to the real. It is a sentiment best reflected in Lovecraft's many letters. In a letter to Farnsworth Wright, his editor at the time of *Weird Tales*,

Lovecraft makes the case for the anti-humanism of his stories: "Now all my tales are based on the fundamental premise that common human laws and interests are emotions that have no validity or significance in the vast cosmos-at-large... but when we cross the line to the boundless and hideous unknown – the shadow-haunted *Outside* – we must remember to leave our humanity and terrestrialism at the threshold."[107]

This is what Lovecraft elsewhere calls "cosmic horror." Cosmic horror positions itself against anthropomorphism – the world regarded in the mytho-poetic shape of the human, the personification of the world as a human world. Cosmic horror also positions itself against anthropocentrism – the world as instrumentally made for the human, the world as a world for human use and benefit.

Thus, at one level Lovecraft's cosmic horror is poised against anthropomorphism, the view of the world in the shape of the human, the world as comprehended precisely because it is in a form that we recognize, either as being like us or as existing in relation to us. The limit of anthropomorphism is therefore the quasi-human, either through personification or in the guise of human-like entities, from pets to robots.

But at another level cosmic horror is against anthropocentrism, the view of the world in relation to human interests, uses, and concerns. Anthropocentrism demands something more than the quasi-human, something more than mere semblance. The limit of anthropocentrism is the non-human, a broad domain that includes objects, assemblages, and things, as well as the hierarchy of animate and inanimate, of higher and lower orders of being, the world of plants and animals.

Cosmic horror – at least in Lovecraft's version – is therefore against both anthropomorphism and anthropocentrism. It would seem that this would leave one option open, that of an antagonism against the human *tout court*, a position generally regarded as misanthropic. In the *mis-anthropos*, the human is either regarded as an accident, an error, or as generally insignificant. It seems that this would leave only a residue that is simply not-human, or better, unhuman.

Now, many tales of supernatural horror not only turn against the human, but they invert anthropomorphism and anthropocentrism, resulting in the misanthropic vision of a malefic and malevolent world. But even this is, in many ways, the ultimate anthropic conceit – the world is against us, but at least it cares enough to take notice. In this inversion, the human attempts to have its cake and to eat it too, tentacles and all. But supernatural horror must move beyond even this misanthropism, into the blank horror of the unhuman, into a region we can only call *indifference*, or what Lovecraft himself referred to as "indifferentism":

> Contrary to what you may assume, I am *not a pessimist* but an *indifferentist* – that is, I don't make the mistake of thinking that the resultant of the natural forces surrounding and governing organic life will have any connexion with the wishes or tastes of any part of that organic life-process. Pessimists are just as illogical as optimists... both schools retain in a vestigial way the primitive concept of a conscious teleology – of a cosmos which gives a damn one way or the other... [the indifferentist] simply knows that this quality has nothing to do with the case; that the interplay of forces which govern climate, behavior, biological growth and decay, and so on, is too purely universal, cosmic, and eternal a phenomenon to have any relationship to the immediate wishing-phenomena of one minute organic species on our transient and insignificant planet... The real philosopher knows that, *other* evidence being equal, favourableness or unfavourableness to mankind means absolutely nothing as an index of likelihood...[108]

In spite of what we may think, Lovecraft's rather awkward term "indifferentism" does not so much indicate a personal predilection towards apathy, boredom, or a general grumpiness. Instead, Lovecraft proposes a diffuse, enigmatic antagonism, an anti-humanism that sets out the parameters for what we might call the "anthropic schema." The anthropic schema is made up of three variants on the human-centric view: anthropomorphism, anthropocentrism, and misanthropy.

Here the world is neither anthropic nor misanthropic, but simply indifferent, an indifference registered by the human in the utter apophatic blackness of incomprehensibility.

*

Black Illumination. This brings us to what is the real issue here, and that is investigating the religious and mystical elements at play in supernatural horror. Lovecraft's shift out of the Kantian and Heideggerian paradigms of horror – that is, from fear to the unknown, from the human to the unhuman – cannot really be appreciated without taking into account the implicit indebtedness of supernatural horror to mystical traditions.

While Lovecraft was a self-described atheist, it is also important to note that much of what is referred to as "mysticism" in the medieval Christian tradition actually ran counter to orthodox Church doctrine. The so-called "negative theology" tradition is a case in point. In the late 5th and early 6th century, Dionysius the Areopagite outlined a distinction between those mystical theologies that drew upon a notion of the divine as fully present (kataphatic or positive theologies), and those that relied on a notion of the divine as shadowy, dark, and absent (apophatic or negative theologies). But as Dionysius takes care to note, the divine is "dark" or "shadowy" not because it is lacking anything, but because it is superlatively beyond human comprehension. The most one can take away from this enigmatic thought is a negative knowledge, the thought of the limit of thought – or to use Lovecraft's phrase, the thought of the "inability of the mind to correlate all its contents."

This logic would be taken further in the tradition of "darkness mysticism," in which the divine is thought through motifs of negation – the desert in Eckhart, the abyss in Ruusbroec, the tomb in Angela of Foligno, darkness in John of the Cross, and the motifs of confusion and obfuscation in *The Cloud of Unknowing*.[109] Such texts lead not to a full comprehension (or even an apprehension) of the divine, but instead to a strange thought that devolves around what Dionysius calls "a negation beyond every assertion," and what Eckhart refers to simply as "the nothingness of God." Such a knowledge is referred to by Dionysius as "unknowing": "By an undivided and absolute abandonment of yourself and everything, shedding all and freed from all, you will be uplifted to the ray of the divine darkness which is above everything that is."[110]

If supernatural horror is indeed driven by this mystical core, then the kind of thinking that takes place in its narratives would have to be akin to the "unknowing" of the apophatic tradition. But supernatural horror is not simply a secular reaffirmation of religious faith. Emphasizing as it does the indifference of the unhuman world, supernatural horror also takes place in a godless world, a world that has been able to encompass both Nietzsche's "death of God" and the return of religious fanaticisms of all types. Disavowing both scientificity and secularism, supernatural horror seems to point to a limit in which there is only the negative without any positive – what Schopenhauer called the *nihil negativum*, or "negative nothingness." So, in so far as supernatural horror is mystical, it would have to be of a heretical type of mysticism, a mysticism without religion, a mysticism without God.

What, then, are we left with? What we're left with is a kind of non-philosophical thought; the thought of the limit of all thought; the thought of the impossibility of thought. It is distinct from thought as reflection – that is, from Descartes' notion of thought as a subject correlated to an object. It is also distinct from thought as access – that is, from Kant's notion of thought as the synthetic tethering of reason, understanding, and sensibility, within an enclosed dyad of self and world. It is, finally, distinct from thought as equivalence – that is, from the Hegelian notion of thought as a continuum between self and world, an equivalence between thought and reality, the rational and the real.

Perhaps it is within frozen thought that we see something different, something on the order of deep time and the scale of the unhuman. Perhaps within frozen thought we really find what we might call a *black illumination*. The black illumination is a degree zero of thought, inaccessible to the senses, unintelligible to thought, impossible to experience – all that is left is the residue of a minimal, frozen thought of an enigmatic epiphany. The black illumination is the *reductio ad absurdum* of philosophy. In the black illumination, thought does not exist, but instead subsists, persists, and even resists. In the black illumination, all experience leads to the impossibility of experience, from the fullness of fear to the emptiness of thought.

We can state it plainly: supernatural horror takes up a set of concerns that have traditionally been the provenance of mysticism and religion. But supernatural horror also operates in a secular, scientific, and skeptical world, and one that ultimately questions the ability of human beings to know anything at all. In so doing, supernatural horror also raises the most basic problems of philosophy. Supernatural horror works against both the Kantian and Heideggerian paradigms, in which the truth of horror is given meaning in fear or in death. Instead, we see a shift from the human-centric concern of emotion and the anxiety towards death, to a strange, unhuman thought beyond even the misanthropic tendency.

If we can accept this, then this allows us to regard supernatural horror in a broader context, one that can incorporate both fictional and non-fictional examples, and allow us to think about supernatural horror beyond genre conventions. It is even possible to construct a history of supernatural horror along these lines. For each period in Western culture, there is a corresponding dichotomy, a kind of governing principle that structures the way horror is manifest as an index of the unknown and the non-human.

For instance, we could say that, for the Middle Ages, the governing principle is that of *showing/hiding*, arrived at via the philosophical method of phenomenology, and expressed in diverse examples such as textual accounts of mystical itineraries, the medieval bestiary, or the treatise on demonology. In each case what is at stake is how something can appear that is in itself not anything. How does the divine or demonic manifest its presence, not being itself substantial?

Likewise, for the Enlightenment, the governing principle is that of *knowing/believing*, or alternately, of reason/faith. Here the phenomena of appearances is less crucial that the cognitive apparatus for producing knowledge from those appearances. The philosophical focus is not phenomenology but epistemology, its exemplars that of the gothic novel, graveyard poetry, on through to the 19th-century horror tale and the literature of decadence. In these examples the presence or absence of the object of horror is secondary to the possibility or impossibility of knowing "what" it is at all.

In the modern period, a whole host of changes in science, technology, and industry provoke another shift, and here the governing principle is a more existential one, that of *thinking/being*. Here the enigmatic and paradoxical nature of the horror leads one into a double-bind: either some "nameless thing" that exists, but which cannot be thought, or some fantastical being that is thought but that cannot exist (at least according to existing laws of nature). The weird tale, the psychic detective genre, and the hybridity of science fiction horror all provide examples in which this thinking/being dichotomy is expressed.

And our own era? It is perhaps too soon to name it, though this has not prevented critics and scholars from posing questions about a postmodern, posthuman era in which all boundaries are dissolved and a fluctuating surface of relative differences proliferates against a non-human backdrop of climate, planet, and cosmos. Perhaps the governing principle is not that of thinking/being, but an even more fundamental one that stretches back to Plato and Parmenides: is there some unifying principle to everything or is there simply the arbitrary existence of what exists? In spite of our persistent attempts to produce theories-of-everything, something always escapes. Thus the governing principle is that of *one/none*; there is something underlying everything, or there is not. Here genres blend, theory becomes fiction, fiction is speculative, and what the cold rationalism of the sciences tell us is more "horrific" than any tale of Lovecraft or Poe. Our own era is one haunted by the shadow of futurity, precisely because there is no future.

But this is not just about the horror genre; it is also a reflection on philosophy, and what happens when the two intersect. For one, philosophy's explanatory function is tripped up, as is its therapeutic function. Rather than a horror of philosophy, in which philosophy would explain or give meaning to horror (the regional, "philosophy of X" approach), horror can be understood to turn back on philosophy, revealing, among other things, a strange, uncanny, apophatic glimmer within philosophy itself. At its limit, supernatural horror challenges philosophy's principle of sufficient reason. Using one of François Laruelle's terms, we might say that horror turns back on philosophy in a non-philosophical way, revealing what Laruelle calls "the philosophical decision," that glimmer that both makes philosophy possible and that is excised from philosophical activity itself.[111] If we were to utilize more precise philosophical language, we could put it this way: *The genre of supernatural horror is an attempt to think the unhuman*, via a philosophical core of the impossibility of all thought.

In supernatural horror, philosophy does not enter in order to explain or even to describe this limit, much less to give it its truth or its meaning. The moment one undertakes anything like a "philosophy of horror," horror turns back on philosophy. Horror uncoils, unwinds, and "bites back," challenging philosophy's most basic presuppositions – the principle of non-contradiction, the principle of sufficient reason, the principle of sufficient philosophy itself. In supernatural horror we see a shift, from the fear of death to the horror of life, from the concern with Being to the indifference of emptiness or nothingness. In supernatural horror, the philosophy of horror is exhumed, turned inside-out, revealing a non-philosophy of horror, or better, the *horror of philosophy*.

*

In Praise of Shadows. Shadows and darkness pervade the most innocuous, everyday objects – a wooden table, a ceramic bowl, a candle, an obscure corner of a room. Sitting at a restaurant in Kyoto, the novelist Jun'ichirō Tanizaki writes:

> The rooms at the Waranjiya are about nine feet square, the size of a comfortable little tearoom, and the alcove pillars and ceilings glow with a faint smoky luster, dark even in the light of the lamp. But in the still dimmer light of the candlestand, as I gazed at the trays and bowls standing in the shadows cast by that flickering point of flame, I discovered in the gloss of this lacquerware a depth and richness like that of a still, dark pond, a beauty I had not before seen.[112]

The bowls and cups, otherwise purely functional objects in a restaurant, suddenly reveal a black and infinite depth that seems to defy the laws of physics. It prompts Tanizaki to think about a world lived by this "darkness seen by candlelight," a world at once readily familiar and yet completely unfathomable: "It must have been simple for specters to appear in a 'visible darkness' where always something seemed to be flickering and shimmering, a darkness that on occasion held greater terrors than darkness out-of-doors."[113]

Such visible darkness is the subject of the short story "Light and Shadows" (1896), by the Russian poet and novelist Fyodor Sologub. It involves a young boy, Volodya and his growing fascination with shadows. It begins, at first, as a harmless children's game, when Volodya discovers a booklet containing instructions for making different types of hand shadows cast on the wall from a light source. Becoming more obsessed with the booklet, Volodya begins to make more shadows with different objects around his desk. He begins to notice shadows everywhere, in his home, at school, on the buildings and street outside. He becomes intrigued by the interplay of light and shadow, how shadow is produced by light and how shadow also negates light. He sees the sun merely as a light source for creating shadows in the daytime. And each night, unable to sleep, he begins his own shadow-play: "These shadowy outlines were becoming near and dear to him. They were not mute – they talked, and Volodya understood their babbling language."[114]

Eventually Volodya's schoolwork suffers, as does his health, and his mother, reprimanding him, takes away the booklet. Volodya finds himself thinking of nothing but shadows, finding them at once alluring and ominous, and finding himself both weary of and fascinated by them:

But the shadows kept haunting him. Even though he didn't summon them with hand-shapes, even though he didn't heap up object upon object so they would make a shadow on the wall, the shadows themselves clustered around him, importunate and insistent... Shadows all around everywhere –

sharply defined ones from lights, dim ones from the dissipated light of day – they all crowded around Volodya, falling across one another, enveloping him in an indissoluble web.[115]

A few nights later, unable to sleep herself, Volodya's mother is found making hand shadows against the parlor wall. "In the dreary moments of morning she searches her soul and thinks back on her life, and she sees that it has been empty, unnecessary, aimless. Nothing more than shadows senselessly flitting by and fading into thickening twilight."[116] In the final scenes of the story both Volodya and his mother are seen casting hand shadows in the night, the rooms of their home lit only by a single lamp, "their joy is hopelessly sorrowful, their sorrow wildly joyful."[117]

In Sologub's story shadow exists in an ambiguous interplay with light, shadow an ambivalent "object" produced by light and cast on a screen-like wall. But in Thomas Ligotti's story "The Shadow, the Darkness" a different notion of shadow is offered to us. The story centers around an art exhibit by one Reiner Grossvogel, a loquacious, sickly aesthete recently released from the local hospital. At the opening of the show Grossvogel gives a speech to preface his new sculptures:

"It is all so very, very simple," the artist continued. "Our bodies are but one manifestation of the energy, the *activating force* that sets in motion all the objects, all the bodies of this world and enables them to exist as they do. This activating force is something like a shadow that is not only the outside of all the bodies of this world but is *inside* of everything and thoroughly pervades everything – an all-moving darkness that has no substance in itself but that moves all the objects of this world, including those objects which we call our bodies..."[118]

Grossvogel then details how, after his hospital episode, he was able to "see" this darkness, this "pervasive shadow" as it subsisted in the world, in each object. And what he sees is not comforting. In itself the shadow of which Grossvogel speaks is insubstantial – it is, literally "no thing." But the shadow is also pervasive and everywhere coursing through everything that exists. Grossvogel's realization is a stark one: "Everywhere I travelled I saw how the pervasive shadow, the all-moving darkness, was *using our world*."[119] Not only can Grossvogel sense this shadow, but he is able to, paradoxically, give it shape in his artwork. The story's description of the sculptures is vague, almost nonsensical. An object at once formless and composed of many forms; a glossy black surface beneath which seemed to swirl other dark shapes; forms suggestive of a creature such as scorpion or crab, and the uncanny suggestion of Grossvogel's body itself.

Near the story's end, a select group of viewers are taken to a site-specific installation, an entire town that seems to exclude darkness and shadow. Eventually the viewers realize that "the shadow" is emerging from within the site itself: "...what we were now seeing was not a darkness descending from far skies but a shadow which was arising from within the dead town around us, as if a torrent of black blood had begun roaring through its pale body."[120] It engulfs the entire site, including the spectators – now unwitting participants. The shape of everything turns "crooked and crabbed, reaching out toward them as if with claws and rising up like strange peaks and horns into the sky, on longer pale and gray but swirling with the pervasive shadow, the all-moving darkness that they could finally see so perfectly because now they were seeing with their bodies, only with their bodies pitched into a great black plain."[121]

Sologub's story imagines shadow existing in some kind of obscure, secret alliance with light, such that shadow can exist even in the middle of the day. By contrast, Ligotti's story imagines a shadow without light, a shadow as primordial as that in Sologub's story, but also metaphysical, as if a kind of dark matter exuding from every apparently substantial, existing thing. These are perversions of Plato's cave, where every light – even the sun outside – exists in order to produce shadows. The shadows become strange things, at once substantial and insubstantial, strange existents at the borderland where matter meets its opposite. In his study *A Short History of the Shadow*, art historian Victor Stoichita notes this strange status of the shadow in modern culture, where the shadow seems to exist of its own accord, with its own mysterious logic and agenda, the shadow as double, as other, as an inner state externalized in the world – "the shadow as an expression of autonomous power."[122] Tethered to light and yet seeming to constantly pull away from it, "[t]he shadow is simultaneously presented as an emanation, a distortion and a projection onto the inner screen of [the] psyche."[123]

To return to our opening points – shadows pervade the most innocuous and everyday of situations. Occasionally we have the opportunity to reflect on these moments. When it is night and I am in a well-lit room, I turn off the lights and, for a moment, it is pitch black. Even though this is a familiar room, and I know that to my right there is a desk, to the left a table, and so on, for a brief moment everything – every thing – vanishes, engulfed by a blackness at once infinite and opaque. For a philosopher like Immanuel Kant, such moments reveal to us how we orient ourselves in the world through our imaginations, though this is not without its own problems:

In the dark I orient myself in a room that is familiar to me if I can take hold of even one single object whose position I remember. But it is plain that nothing helps me here except the faculty for determining position according to a *subjective* ground of differentiation: for I do not see all the objects whose place I am to find; and if someone as a joke had moved all the object around so that what was previously on the right was now on the left, I would be quite unable to find anything in a room whose walls were otherwise wholly identical.[124]

A more terrifying version of this joke is given in an episode of the radio show *Lights Out!*, entitled simply "The Dark." Originally aired on December 29th, 1937, this short episode features a policeman and doctor en route to a remote house, responding to an emergency call. They arrive only to find a dark, seemingly abandoned old house. They open the inevitably creaky door, and inside they find a cackling old woman, and an unrecognizable mass of flesh, which they soon realize is a man – turned inside out. But this is only the beginning of their horrors. They open a further door, but this opens not to another room, but to... nothing. They shine a flashlight in, but the light does not reflect against any surface, floor, wall, or ceiling. "I don't see nothin' but dark... the dark sorta spills over on the edges..." the policeman says. Another room, and the same thing. The house seems to be built of infinite, expansive darkness. As the doctor says, peering into the endlessly black room: "Well, look I tell ya – it's a deeper dark than... dark..." Eventually they notice something moving in the dark, but this is, strangely, the dark itself. It pours out and envelops the old woman, turning her body inside out. Aghast and speechless, the policeman and doctor are frozen in terror: "The shadows – they're crawling on the floor towards us..."[125]

*

Black Matheme. It usually starts with something small, something innocuous, a little obsession. You become fascinated by something you see, something that catches your eye: a particular pattern on a tablecloth, the shape of snail shells, the inward curve of a plant's tendrils, the shape in a ceramic cup, the swirling motion of your miso soup. Your interest is piqued, and "hm, that's interesting" gradually becomes "what else can I learn about it?" The focal point expands, gradually and by steps, until it eclipses your view of the world entirely, overlapping with it perfectly. And then, ever so slightly, the little obsession becomes a big obsession, and soon everything is made of spirals, from microscopic cells and granules of sand to the human settlement patterns outside of cities, massive hurricane cloud formations, the galaxies, even thought itself.

This is the trajectory of Junji Ito's manga series *Uzumaki*, published between 1998 and 1999.[126] It begins as we follow two teenagers who witness their home town of Kurôzu-cho become obsessed by the shape of the spiral, eventually driving them all to murder, madness, or suicide. The "spiral obsession" appears to spread through the town, affecting not only the townspeople, but manifesting itself in the materiality of the town itself. An abstraction is suddenly rampant everywhere, from the spiral-shaped grass on the hillside to the swirling black fumes of cremated bodies. Ceramics, soup, hair, clothing, even the town itself, arrayed in a spiral-shaped row of houses, become so many material vehicles for the spiral. By the third volume, the town of Kurôzu-cho has become a massive spiral dwelling, composed of the bodies of its inhabitants.

As an abstract geometric shape, the spiral is, in itself, nothing. It is only given presence by being manifest in some thing – a cup, a plant, a snail shell; even a drawing of a spiral requires the material substrate of ink and paper. Throughout *Uzumaki* we almost never see an abstract spiral, the spiral is always some thing. And yet, the spiral spreads throughout the town, crossing boundaries between the living and non-living, organic and inorganic, animal, plant, or mineral. The spiral is not reducible to any of those incarnations – but it is not separate from them either. What drives many of the townspeople mad is this duplicity – the tangible presence of the spiral matched with its intangible abstractness. It appears to be everywhere and nowhere, a black matheme that spreads even into the very thoughts of the characters themselves.

In the penultimate chapter of the series – titled, simply, "Galaxy" – a mild-mannered astronomy teacher appears to have discovered a new galaxy, which is – you guessed it – strangely spiral-shaped. But the galaxy is more than that; it appears to have spirals upon spirals of star-stuff folding in on itself. "Such strange luminosity... such crooked arms... It really is a weird galaxy." What's more, the spiral galaxy seems to emit "transmissions" to the astronomy teacher. By the end of the story he has turned into a raving lunatic, his eyes sunken in a spiral shape, driven mad by the incessant signals coming to him from the spiral galaxy. And his students seem to discover more and more spiral galaxies, none of them previously recorded. At one point, the astronomy teacher offers himself before the night sky, the spiral galaxies now visible to the naked eye, and beckons to the spiral galaxy to take him. A moment later a flash of light either emanates down from the sky or from within the teacher's head. "After exploding like an egg in a microwave, Torino's head turned into a small galaxy and flew off into the night sky."[127] But, as with the spiral shape itself, the end is not really the end: "And it will be the same moment when it ends again... When the next

Kurôzu-cho is built amidst the ruins of the old one... When the eternal spiral awakes once more..."[128]

At the center of Ito's manga series is an inversion that takes place between the human being and an enigmatic something else that constitutes a horizon for human thought. Let us call this "something else" the *unhuman*. The unhuman is not simply that which is not human, be it animals, machines, oceans, or cities, though all of these play a role in Ito's story. The unhuman is also not that which is made human, in which we would have featherless, bipedal walking and talking spirals – though even this is hinted at in *Uzumaki* as well. The unhuman is distinct from these two ways of thinking – anthropocentrism and anthropomorphism, respectively.

What then is the unhuman? It is, first of all, a limit without reserve, something that one is always arriving at, but which is never circumscribed within the ambit of human thought. In a story like *Uzumaki*, we see at least four stages by which one encounters the unhuman. At the first level, we encounter the unhuman only as it exists for the human. This is the normative world of modern suburban living described by the teenagers Shuichi and Kirie at the beginning of the story. At this level, the unhuman is everything that is for us and for our benefit as human beings, living in human cultures, and bearing some unilateral and instrumental relation to the world around us. Houses, rivers, the countryside, roads, people, occupations, schools, hospitals, and the like. This relation between human and unhuman relies upon an *anthropic subversion*. The unhuman is only that which exists within the scope of the human; in a sense, there is no outside of the human, in so far as the unhuman is always fully encompassed by human knowledge and technics. At this level, the unhuman is everything that is subject to and produced by human knowledge. At this level, anthropocentrism overlaps almost perfectly with anthropomorphism.

But *Uzumaki* steadily moves towards a second level, which reintroduces a notion of the unhuman through an inversion of the relation between human and unhuman. Rather than a merely subjective obsession, the spiral manifests itself in the physical surroundings of Kurôzu-cho itself – as if the spiral were "interested" in the townspeople of Kurôzu-cho. Note that a relation of unilateralism still exists, except that it has been reversed. Instead of human beings making use of the world for their own ends, the world is revealed to be making use of human beings for its own end. Humans are simply a way for the spiral to produce and reproduce itself, be it as grass, clouds, bodies, or galaxies. Clearly, with this sort of epiphany, all bets are off – one can no longer regard the human endeavors of science, technology, and art in quite the same way. But the terms of this relation are still human – intentionality, instrumental rationality, and even a touch of malice are attributed to the abstraction of the spiral. It is as if the unhuman can only be understood through the lens of the human. We can call this the *anthropic inversion*. The anthropic inversion allows for a concept of the unhuman to emerge, but it is ultimately recuperated within the ambit of human categories, such as intelligence and intentionality.

Towards the end of *Uzumaki*, this undergoes another turn, leading to a third level at which the unhuman is encountered. As the astronomy teacher is violently and weirdly carried off into the spiral night where flesh and geometry merge into one, his own individuation slips away and is engulfed, and at this moment we realizes that the human categories of living/non-living, human/non-human are themselves simply one manifestation of the unhuman. In other words, as opposed to the anthropic inversion (humans don't make spirals, spirals make us), here the townspeople of Kurôzu-cho experience another kind of inversion, an *ontogenic inversion* in which everything human is revealed to be one instance of the unhuman. The ontogenic inversion is both ontological and ontogenetic, at once the evisceration of thought from the human, and an epiphany about the essentially unhuman qualities of the human.

At this point thought falters, and here we enter a fourth stage that we can call *misanthropic subtraction*. Language can only continue by way of an apophatic use of negative terms ("nameless," "formless," "lifeless"), which themselves are doomed to failure. This failure is leveraged with great effect in the literary tradition of supernatural horror and weird fiction. Authors such as Clark Ashton Smith, Frank Belknap Long, and of course H.P. Lovecraft excelled at driving language to this breaking point. Here one notices two strategies that are regularly used, often in concert with each other. There is a strategy of minimalism, in which language is stripped of all its attributes, leaving only skeletal phrases such as "the nameless thing," "the shapeless thing," or "the unnamable," which is also the title of a Lovecraft story. There is also a strategy of hyperbole, in which the unknowability of the unhuman is expressed through a litany of baroque descriptors, all of which ultimately fail to inscribe the unhuman within human thought and language. Some examples from Lovecraft include:

...the rayless gloom with Miltonic legions of the misshapen damned...
...the nameless bands of abhorrent elder-world hierophants...
...brooding, half-material, alien Things that festered in earth's nether abysses...
...a pandeamoniae vortex of loathsome sound and utter, materially tangible blackness...

Often these two strategies dovetail into a singular epiphany concerning the faltering not just of language, but of thought as well. At the end of Lovecraft's story "The Unnamable," one of the characters, speaking to his friend Carter from a hospital bed, attempts to describe his strange experience in the following way:

No – it wasn't that way at all. It was everywhere – a gelatin – a slime – yet it had shapes, a thousand shapes of horror beyond all memory. There were eyes – and a blemish. It was the pit – the maelstrom – the ultimate abomination. Carter, *it was the unnamable!*[129]

Taken together, these four stages result in a paradoxical revelation, in which one thinks the thought of the limit of all thought. At the level of the anthropic subversion – the first stage – this limit is present but hidden, occulted, and remains unrecognized. At the level of the anthropic inversion – the second stage – this limit is brought into the foreground through a reversal of the terms, but not of the relation. But even here the unhuman remains a limit, something only known at best indirectly, through the ad-hoc use of human terms (such as sentience or intentionality or malice). Proceeding from this, at the third level the ontogenic inversion produces a misanthropic realization, a realization that the unhuman exists antagonistically with respect to the human. This leads to the fourth stage, the misanthropic subtraction, in which the relation itself is reversed. Here the unhuman is not even known indirectly – and yet it is still intuited, still thought, but only via a thought that has been stripped of all its attributes. What is thought is only this absolute inaccessibility, this absolute incommensurability; what is affirmed is only that which is negation.

What results, then, is not just human knowledge and its relative horizon of the thinkable, but an enigmatic revelation of the unthinkable – what we've already termed a *black illumination*. It leads from the human to the unhuman, but it is also already the unhuman, or one instance of the unhuman. Black illumination does not lead to the affirmation of the human within the unhuman, but instead opens onto the *indifference* of the unhuman. The unhuman does not exist for us (the humanism of the unhuman), and neither is it against us (the misanthropy of the unhuman). Black illumination leads to the enigmatic thought of the immanence of indifference. The unhuman, at its limit, becomes identical with a kind of apophatic indifference towards the human – at the same time that this indifferent unhuman is immanently "within" the human as well. It is, no doubt, for this reason that the examples of black illumination in supernatural horror indelibly bear the mark of a generalized misanthropy, that moment when philosophy and horror negate themselves, and in the process become one and the same.

*

Naturhorror. Near the end of the 18th century, the German philosopher, novelist, and aphorist Friedrich Schelling sought to formulate a renewed philosophy of nature that would combine the findings of the physical sciences with that of speculative philosophy in the wake of Immanuel Kant. Kant's critical philosophy had forged a wedge between the world in itself and our perception of the world, but post-Kantian thinkers like Schelling sought ways of bridging Kant's division of self and world. For Schelling, the key intuition was that the self that thinks about the world is also part of the world, and it is a mistake to presume that there is first a separately existing self that then turns towards and reflects on the world as an object. The world that the self thinks about is also "in" the self, and the two share something in common that may not be reducible to either.

What, then, is that "something" that is common to both self and world? For Schelling, "nature" came to signify that commonality – but by nature Schelling does not mean "the outdoors" or forests and oceans, and neither does he mean nature in the sense of a fixed essence (as in "human nature"). Nature for Schelling was that "something" that was not in itself anything, a unity without boundary constituted entirely of process, becoming, flux and flow – a "ground" of the world that was also continually ungrounding itself. In his study *Philosophies of Nature After Schelling*, Iain Hamilton Grant encapsulates this intuition: "Self-conscious subjectivity, therefore, is simply the 'highest power' of the 'identity of subjective and objective we call nature.'"[130] The stakes of such a philosophy are high, as Grant summarizes:

If, in other words, "to philosophize about nature means to create nature," the latter cannot be a nature restricted apriori by the particular physiological means by which it philosophizes. Instead, nature philosophizing must itself be unconditioned, so that the range of instances of natural philosophy must extend beyond the remit of physiologically conditioned particulars such as species, or even phylla.[131]

In his experimental and syncretic approach, Schelling incorporated ideas from physics, biology, geology, chemistry, as well as elements from mystical theology and classical myth. Given the questions Schelling is posing, such a philosophy would no longer simply be a philosophy *of* nature, as if the philosopher stood above and apart from nature. For if the nature that I am thinking about is also in me and coursing through me, then it follows that I am in some way identical with nature, and that nature "thinks" me just as I think nature. As Grant puts it, "what thinks in me is what is outside me." Instead of a philosophy of nature, Schelling proposes a *naturphilosophie*. Thought becomes strangely impersonal and non-human, just as the human subject becomes at once the one who thinks nature and that which is thought by and through nature.

But if this is the case, and what thinks in me is also outside me, it is also possible that what is outside me is also outside of my individual, subjective concerns, hopes, and desires, just as what thinks in me is also alien, impersonal, and similarly estranged to the "me" that is thought. My thoughts are not my own, and I am thought by an enigmatic non-entity whose motives may be contrary to my own – or which may have no motives at all. Contra Schelling's romantic conception of the unity of self and world, the nature in me and the nature outside me, there is another kind of "nature," one that courses through self and world, but that does so without aim or end, indifferent to the self's possessive individualism and the species' sense of superiority. What thinks in me is what is outside me. Is this not also a description of "nature" as invasive, contagious, over-running the human being like some kind of overgrown and dilapidated ruin? Would this not transform Schelling's *naturphilosophie* into a *naturhorror*?

Among authors of supernatural horror, no one has examined the role of nature more than Algernon Blackwood. In story after story Blackwood's characters discover a nature that is a darker version of Schelling's *naturphilosophie,* and a nature that they are, at the same time, drawn to, often undergoing ambivalent transformations. Lyrical and foreboding, Blackwood's story "The Man Whom the Trees Loved" (1912) tells of a husband and wife enjoying their cabin in the woods. Gradually the husband becomes more and more interested in the trees that surround their house, taking long walks in the forest, himself becoming more and more silent and preoccupied. He dreams of the slow, swaying, forest trees, and his dreams begin to blur into his daily life. The couple can't tell, but it seems as if the trees outside their house have moved ever so imperceptibly closer. At night, amid the "strong smell of mould and fallen leaves" the wife feels a presentment of something close but intangible, something linked to the trees outside: "The horrible, dim enchantment of the trees was close about them in the room – gnarled, ancient, lonely trees of winter, whispering round the human life they loved."[132] One night, amid stirring dreams, the wife suddenly awakes. There are wet leaves and dew on her clothing, as if she had been outside.

In the dim, moonlit darkness, she glances over at her husband, sound asleep. Then she looks up:

> …what caught her unawares was the horrid thing that by this fact of a sudden, unexpected waking she had surprised these other things in the room, beside the very bed, gathered close about him while he slept… She screamed before she realised what she did – a long, high shriek of terror that filled the room, yet made so little actual sound. For wet and shimmering presences stood grouped all round that bed. She saw their outline underneath the ceiling, the green, spread bulk of them, their vague extension over walls and furniture. They shifted to and fro, massed yet translucent, mild yet thick, moving and turning within themselves to a hushed noise of multitudinous soft rustling. In their sound was something very sweet and winning that fell into her with a spell of horrible enchantment.[133]

Seamlessly crossing nature outside and nature inside, waking and dreaming, the animate and inanimate, the eerie forest trees in Blackwood's story literally envelop the characters in an intimate, lulling terror, a "horrible enchantment" that pulls the human characters further and further away from the human.

Something similar happens in Kyōka Izumi's story "The Holy Man of Mount Kōya" (1900), which tells the story of a young Buddhist monk making his way to a monastery near the mountain, and the various events that occur along the way. The monk begins his journey on a road, which then turns to a path, which then vanishes, leaving the monk directionless as he walks into a dense forest. He sees a snake, various insects, and at one point discovers a leech on his arm. Then, inexplicably, a torrent of leeches descends upon him from the trees. Fatigued, delirious, and panic-striken, "it was then," the monk states, "that the strangest thought occurred to me": "These terrifying mountain leeches had been gathered there since the age of the gods, lying in wait for passersby... And at the same time, all these enormous trees, large enough to block out even the midday sun, will break into small pieces that will then turn into even more leeches..."[134] Foreboding in its appearance, the forest through which the monk walks literally takes on animalistic properties, the boundary between vegetable, animal, and mineral passing away. Recalling the experience later, the monk solemnly observes:

> The destruction of mankind will not come with the rupture of the earth's fragile crust and with fire pouring down from the heavens. Nor will it come when the waves of the ocean wash over the land. Rather, it will begin with the forests of Hida turning into leeches and end with black creatures swimming in blood and muck. Only then will a new generation of life begin.[135]

This intermingling of forms is at the center of a group of short stories by the contemporary horror author and paleontologist Caitlín R. Kiernan. Published in her 2000 collection *Tales of Pain and Wonder*, each of the stories focuses on a particular place where some undefined scientific anomaly is accidentally discovered. In the story "In the Water Works (Birmingham, Alabama 1888)," it is the construction and mining site near Red Mountain, at the tip of the Appalachias. There, geology teacher Henry S. Matthews carries out his research under the auspices of the Birmingham Water Works and the Elyton Land Companies, gathering samples, accumulating data, a northerner minding his own business down south. Eventually the miners discover what appears to be a massive fault within the mountain. The foreman asks Matthews to come with them to take a look. As they go deeper and deeper into the mountain, Matthews notices a strange, repulsive, rotten stench, the stench, he thinks of dark, fungoid, mold-ridden rocks. When they finally arrive at the breach, Matthews, still repulsed by the smell, isn't sure what he sees: "...a wide crevice in the wall of the tunnel maybe four feet across and dropping suddenly away into darkness past the reach of the lantern, running west into more blackness but pinching closed near the tunnel's ceiling."[136] The foreman holds Matthews' arm as he slowly leans over into the blackness. He discovers the bottom of the cavern is flooded, the black water infinitely deep. Looking closer, the foreman still holding him, Matthews notices something else:

> At first he doesn't see anything, angle a little less than ninety degrees where black rock meets blacker water, and then he does see something and thinks it must be the roots of some plant growing in the pool, or, more likely, running down from the forest above to find this hidden moisture. Gnarled roots as big around as his arm, twisted wood knotted back on itself... But one of them moves, then, abrupt twitch as it rolls away from the others...[137]

Matthews watches in dismay as one of the roots rises out of the water, and, dripping, glides slowly towards him – and on its underside there is a small, fossil-like worm, "coiling and uncoiling, and here are a thousand of them, restless polyps sprouting from this greater appendage, row upon writhing row, and now it's risen high enough that the thing is right in front of him, shimmering in the lantern light, a living question mark..."[138]

That question mark is at the center of both the horror genre and philosophy. It demands to be taken both literally and figuratively. And it is a question mark posed to the sciences as well. This is something that American author and purveyor of the paranormal Charles Fort knew well. In a string of books published between 1919 and 1932, Fort, spending hours upon hours in the New York Public Library, amassed material on unexplained phenomena. Scientific papers, philosophy books, news reports, travelogues, even anecdotal accounts – nothing escaped from Fort's keen eye, as he gathered data on those phenomena which had been excluded from the existing scientific and philosophical systems. Some of his books gathered together data relating to biological anomalies, while others pertained to geological anomalies, and still others to cosmological anomalies. At the center of his project lay a deep interest in the limits of human knowledge:

> All attempted organizations and systems and consistencies, some approximating far higher than others, but all only intermediate to Order and Disorder, fail eventually because of their relations with outside forces. All are attempted completenesses. If to all local phenomena there are always outside forces, these attempts, too, are realizable only in the state of completeness, or that to which there are no outside forces.[139]

Such phenomena were that portion of knowledge, that which must be excluded in order for systematic knowledge and natural laws to exist at all. His books read less like coherent theories and more like a compendium of facts and figures put in narrative form, the "data of the damned." A deep-seated skepticism undergirds Fort's books: "Nothing has ever been defined. Because there is nothing to define."[140] Or: "Nothing has ever been finally found out. Because there is nothing to find out."[141] Or again: "We are not realists. We are not idealists. We are intermediatists – that nothing is real, but that nothing is unreal: that all phenomena are approximations one way or the other between realness and unrealness."[142] What Fort attempted in works like *The Book of the Damned* was nothing less than a "procession of data that Science has excluded." At the same time, Fort's books are mostly absent of any conclusions, his authorial voice in the selection and juxtaposition of "damned" facts, as if "the facts themselves" revealed things far more horrific and unmentionable than the fancies of a writer's imagination.

*

An Exegesis on Tentacles. There is never just one tentacle, but many. And yet, the many tentacles always seem to trail off into nothing, into a distant ocean abyss as black as the ink it secretes. The cephalopod occupies this duality, a multiplicity of seemingly incongruous features – tentacles and multiple "arms" with suckers, a razor-sharp "beak," a complex nervous system, rows of intestinal "teeth," and a formless "head" – whose coherence falls apart once one tries to make sense of the whole creature. Emerging from a lightless ocean depth, the tentacles seem to lead back down to the abyss from which they came, a multiplicity dissipating into a slumberous, slow, and alien depth. When the tentacles are not reaching down, they are reaching up, for prey – fish, crustaceans, a whale, a sea-borne ship, a flailing human body. This is the cultural mythos, at least. From medieval Icelandic fables of the Kraken, to Jules Verne's *20,000 Leagues Beneath the Sea*, tentacles envelop human beings in their unhuman embrace, the abyss of the unknown sea reaching up to the surface with a certain inevitability.

At the same time, cephalopods are products of human knowledge-production. We have given them their various names, both scientific and colloquial, and they make appearances in the natural history works of Pliny the Elder and Linnaeus, as well as in the Teuthological studies of modern marine biologists. This has not, however, prevented the periodic and often dubious reports of giant squids, which continue to this day. At once products of science and myth, a multiplicity receding into an abyss, an alien creature become like a god – these are themes woven into China Miéville's 2010 novel *Kraken*, his own rendition of cephalopod-lore.

Like many of Miéville's novels, the backdrop of *Kraken* is urban London. But counterposed to this is the vast sea. One is bustling with noise, the other enigmatically silent. One is built up or broken down, the other flows, sometimes turbulently and sometimes imperceptibly. In the interzone between city and sea *Kraken* introduces us to a whole bestiary of groups and organizations – the London Natural History Museum, the Darwin Centre, the FSRC (Fundamentalist and Sect-Related Crime Unit), the Krakenist cult, Londonmancers, the Brotherhood of the Blessed Flood, Knuckleheads, Gunfarmers, Chaos Nazis, and other nefarious grifters, gangsters, and cultists, each warring for their own apocalypse. Caught in the middle of it all is Billy Harrow, ex-student and curator at the Natural History Museum. But running through everything is the enigmatic and mute figure of the giant cephalopod, encased in museum glass as visitors gaze at it with an equal muteness.

All-touching, all-seeing, an alien intelligence writing with an ink illegible but in the sea, in *Kraken* the cephalopod becomes at once an object of religion and of science – an object of religion because of science. Beneath the all-too-human veneer of urban London patterns emerge, linking city, sea, and the unhuman forms of life that pass between them. As one character notes, "What was squiddity but otherness, incomprehensibility. Why would such a deity understand those bent on its glory? Why should it offer anything? Anything at all?"[143] An old Londonmancer, deciphering the bloody entrails of a cut-open city concrete, gives a foreboding reading: "Everything closing down. Something coming up."[144]

But if, for these fringe groups, the cephalopod has become a god, it is not an anthropomorphic or even communicative god. In the library of the Krakenist cult, in a concrete bunker deep underground, Billy discovers a storehouse of "cephalopod folklore" – *Moby Dick*, Jules Verne, poems by Hugh Cook and

Tennyson, obscure scientific papers, and secret treatises such as the dreaded *Apocrypha Tentacula*. In one of the books he reads:

> We cannot see the universe. We are in the darkness of a trench, a deep cut, dark water heavier than earth, presences lit by our own blood, little biolumes, heroic and pathetic. Promethei too afraid or weak to steal fire but able to still glow. Gods are among us and they care nothing and are nothing like us. This is how we are brave: we worship them anyway.[145]

In *Kraken*, the alterity of the cephalopod is matched only by its indifference towards the various groups that attempt to interpret it, and thus to control it. Eventually the enigma of the cephalopod becomes the enigma of the sea itself. At one point in the novel Billy visits the Brotherhood of the Blessed Flood, who protect an oracle of the sea. But the sea remains impervious to human demands. Billy muses:

> The sea is neutral. The sea didn't get involved in intrigues, didn't take sides in London's affairs. Wasn't interested. Who the hell could understand the sea's motivations, anyway? And who would be so lunatic as to challenge it? No one could fight that. You don't go to war against a mountain, against lightning, against the sea. It had its own counsel, and petitioners might sometimes visit its embassy, but that was for their benefit, not its. The sea was not concerned: that was the starting point.[146]

The starting point is, then, this indifference of the world. It is an insight found not only myths and fables but in the treatises of natural history and science. Commenting on the myriad of monsters in the sea, physician Ambroise Paré notes, in his 16th-century *On Monsters and Marvels* (*Des Monstres et Prodiges*), that "awesome things likewise happen on water. For huge flames of fire spreading across the water have been seen issuing from the abysses and whirlpools of the sea – a very monstrous thing – as if the great quantity of water could not stifle the fire; in this God shows himself incomprehensible, as in all his works."[147]

Whether one puts it in the language of fiction or of science, the result is the same – the sudden realization of a stark, "tentacular" alienation from the world in which one is enmeshed. For these and other texts the cephalopod stands in as a manifestation of that indifference of the black, inky abyss. And in a modern context it is largely through scientific knowledge-production that this tentacular alienation is made possible. We human beings are, after all, the ones who have dreamed up taxonomies, anatomies, and nomenclatures, making possible the most systematic, rigorous articulation of this alienation. In a sense, the result of scientific classification is not that we as human beings finally find our place in the world, but the reverse – that we increasingly feel ill-at-ease in the world. It is we who are alien.

This is the insight of *Vampyroteuthis Infernalis*, an incomparable and strange work that straddles the line between science and fiction, biology and horror. Published in the 1980s by the philosopher and journalist Vilém Flusser, the *Vampyroteuthis* is written in the language of a biological classification textbook or a marine biology research paper. Appended to it is a report by the Scientific Institute for Paranaturalist Research, a set of anatomical illustrations and accompanying text, both by the artist Louis Bec. The text details the purported discovery of a new species of hyper-complex, "intelligent" cephalopod, dubbed *Vampyroteuthis infernalis* due to its many rows of undulating teeth and the general "voracity of their expression." As a whole, the *Vampyroteuthis* text is a study in self-reflexivity; the language of biological classification is not simply mocked but respectfully, even enthusiastically employed, to give the reader a sense of the strangeness of much of life on the planet. The cephalopod is the key figure in the text, at once the most remote from the human being, and yet, as Flusser contends, at the same time uncannily near to us:

>...the vampyroteuthis is not entirely alien to us. The abyss that separates us is incomparably smaller than that which separates us from extraterrestrial life... We are pieces of the same game, both constructed of genetic information, and we belong to a branch of the same phylogenetic tree to which its branch belongs. Our common ancestors dominated the beaches of the earth for millions of years, and it was relatively late in the history of life that our paths began to diverge...[148]

For all its playfulness, at the center of the *Vampyroteuthis* report is this theme of relating to a form of life radically unhuman. As Flusser notes "without any previous knowledge of biology, we feel a sense of belonging to our phylum whenever we step on a mollusk, on the one hand, or when we hear, on the other, a crackling bone under our shoe. We feel a connection with life-forms supported by bones, while other forms of life disgust us." This leads Flusser to the evocative idea of a "biological existentialism": "Though existential philosophy has concerned itself with the idea of disgust, it has never attempted to formulate a category of 'biological existentialism,' to advance something like the following hypothesis: 'Disgust recapitulates phylogenesis.'"[149]

Disgust recapitulates phylogenesis. Here Flusser is playing on the truism of genetics, "ontogeny recapitulates phylogeny," which argues that the development of the individual organism replays the evolutionary development of its species. Flusser applies this to the affective domain of disgust, so beloved by existentialist thinkers such as Sartre and Camus. Later in the text Flusser gives a more tangible definition: "The more disgusting something is, the further removed it is from humans on the phylogenetic tree."[150] The insight of the science of biological classification is, Flusser suggests, to have articulated in great detail the scope and range of human disgust towards that which is not human.

Such disgust is also, of course, a sign of the human being's failure to appreciate or relate to that which is not human, other than in terms of utility for us as human beings. This is especially evident in the many horror tales featuring cephalopods, kraken, giant squids, and other nefarious sea creatures, from the *Orlando Furioso* to the tales of nautical horror by the likes of Edgar Allan Poe and William Hope Hodgson. A case in point is the H.P. Lovecraft short story "Dagon," published in 1919. The plot of the story is threadbare, and found in many of Lovecraft's tales – an unnamed narrator tells of his being lost in a strange and terrifying place, and of the unmentionable things he sees there, which, of course, no one believes once he returns home, driving him to the brink of madness. Disgust pervades the story, from the narrator's first impressions of the strange "island": "When at last I awaked, it was to discover myself half sucked into a slimy expanse of hellish black mire which extended about me in monotonous undulations as far as I could see, and in which my boat lay grounded some distance away... The region was putrid with the carcasses of decaying fish, and of other less describable things which I saw protruding from the nasty mud of the unending plain."[151] Lost without compass or map, shipwrecked and delirious, the impression leads the narrator into the depths of cosmic horror: "Perhaps I should not hope to convey in mere words the unutterable hideousness that can dwell in absolute silence and barren immensity."[152]

Though the island appears uninhabited, the remnants of what he does discover make no sense within the ambit of existing human history, archaeology, and science. It is unclear if the "island" is a recent upheaval of rock from a deep sea volcano. A deep ravine leads to a dark pool and a giant, black, "Cyclopean

monolith," covered in strange symbols and depictions of unrecognizable creatures, all unmistakably sculpted by some unnamed
and unseen entity.

"Then suddenly I saw it." Something "loathsome" rising to
the surface of dark waters, sliding into partial view, a
"stupendous monster of nightmares," "gigantic scaly arms"
reaching around the monolith, a "hideous" and bowed head,
emitting "certain measured sounds." "I think I went mad then."

The narrator's frantic escape and rescue does not console him.
He is tainted with an anthropocentric disgust that will not leave
him, and the only thing he is disgusted by more than
cephalopod-like creatures from the deep is his own species,
unable to comprehend a world both alien and indifferent to the
human perspective:

> I cannot think of the deep sea without shuddering at the
> nameless things that may at this very moment be crawling and
> floundering on its slimy bed, worshipping their ancient stone
> idols and carving their own detestable likenesses on
> submarine obelisks or water-soaked granite. I dream of a day
> when they may rise above the billows to drag down in their
> reeking talons the remnants of puny, war-exhausted mankind
> – of a day when the land shall sink, and the dark ocean floor
> shall ascend amidst universal pandemonium.[153]

His final words, at once a prayer and indictment.

*

We Are Not From Here (Ligotti). The idea of an American
pessimism is an oxymoron. In a culture that thrives on entrepre-
neurialism, pharmacology, and self-help, "pessimism" is simply
a fancy name for a bad mood. In a culture that prizes the can-do,
self-starter attitude, to be a pessimist is simply to be a complainer

– if you're not part of the solution, then you're part of the problem. To live in such a culture is to constantly live in the shadow of an obligatory optimism, a novel type of coercion that is pathologized early on in child education in the assessment: "Does not like to play with others."

If one were to compile a list of contemporary American pessimists, the list would be short, though Thomas Ligotti's name would likely be on it. To most who are familiar with his work, Ligotti is known as an author of horror fiction. His 1986 debut *Songs of a Dead Dreamer* immediately set him apart from his contemporaries. Filled with dark, lyrical prose, it displayed an unabashed appreciation for the tradition of the gothic. It was composed of short texts that were difficult to categorize, and that barely contained narrative and plot. When it was published, *Songs of a Dead Dreamer* stood in direct contrast to much horror fiction of the 1980s, which was mostly characterized by slasher-style gore and violence, and a more brutalist approach to language. Ligotti's writing, by contrast, tended more towards an effusive, contorted prose that revealed almost nothing – though each of his pieces was steeped in a somber, funeral mood more reminiscent of the "supernatural horror" tradition of Edgar Allan Poe and H.P. Lovecraft. All the horrors – the real horrors – remained hidden in a stark, unhuman nether region beyond all comprehension, and yet instilled directly in the flesh of the narrators or characters.

In a career that spans almost thirty years, Ligotti's work has remained committed to this tradition of supernatural horror, and, given the trends, fads, and wild mood swings of the horror genre, such a commitment is an admirable anomaly. Which brings us to Ligotti's most recent book, *The Conspiracy Against the Human Race* (hereafter *Conspiracy*). Fans of Ligotti's writing may find this book puzzling at first. For one, it is not a work of horror fiction; for that matter, it's not a work of fiction at all. But to call it a collection of essays or a treatise of philosophy doesn't quite do it justice either. Ligotti does comment at length on the horror genre and on a number of authors, from Anne Radcliffe and Joseph Conrad to Poe and Lovecraft. But *Conspiracy* is not just a writer's personal opinion of other writers. Similarly, Ligotti does spend much of the book reflecting on pessimism, reminding us of the freshness of grumpy thinkers like Arthur Schopenhauer, while also pointing to more obscure or forgotten thinkers, such as the Norwegian philosopher and alpinist Peter Wessel Zapffe. But Ligotti's approach is much too eccentric and uncompromising to be considered academic philosophy, and as a book *Conspiracy* is unencumbered by reams of footnotes or jargon-heavy vocabulary. Finally, Ligotti does address a number of topical issues in *Conspiracy* – research in cognitive neuroscience, the natalism/ anti-natalism debate, global warming and overpopulation, transhumanism, Terror Management Therapy, the popularity of Buddhism, and the self-help boom, among others. But the aim of the book is not simply to be topical, nor to present a "pop" introduction to a difficult topic.

So then, what kind of book is *Conspiracy*? It is first and foremost a book about pessimism; but it is also a pessimistic book. While it contains critical insights into the heights and pitfalls of pessimist thinking, it also contains stunning indictments of our many pretentions to being human: "As for us humans, we reek of our own sense of being something special"; "What is most uncanny about the self is that no one has yet been able to present the least evidence of it."[154] *Conspiracy* constantly hovers around that boundary between writing *about* pessimism and simply *writing* pessimism, and nowhere is this more evident than in Ligotti's own brand of pessimism, which is at once uncompromising and absurd:

> Nature proceeds by blunders; that is its way. It is also ours. So if we have blundered by regarding consciousness as a blunder, why make a fuss over it? Our self-removal from this

planet would still be a magnificent move, a feat so luminous it would bedim the sun. What do we have to lose? No evil would attend our departure from this world, and the many evils we have known would go extinct along with us. So why put off what would be the most laudable masterstroke of our existence, and the only one?[155]

Different though it is from his previous work, *Conspiracy* is very much a Ligotti book, both in style and in the ideas it contains. In fact, I would argue that *Conspiracy* is the logical next step in Ligotti's trajectory as a writer. While the book is "philosophical" in a general sense, in reading *Conspiracy* one gets the feeling that Ligotti has pushed the boundaries of horror fiction to the limit, where the next step would be to abandon the fictional elements altogether, dispensing with narrative, character, and plot, in favor of the *ideas* of horror fiction. It is not difficult to see a continuum stretching from the short, abstract mood pieces of Edgar Allan Poe, to Lovecraft's "documentary" approach to horror, to a generation of post-war horror authors such as Ramsey Campbell. Lovecraft himself noted this in his 1927 essay *Supernatural Horror in Literature*, where he argues for an understanding of the horror genre in terms of thought – and the limits of thought – more than character, setting, or plot. It is an approach that, as Ligotti notes, characterizes nearly all supernatural horror fiction: "In the literature of supernatural horror, a familiar storyline is that of a character who encounters a paradox *in the flesh*, so to speak, and must face down or collapse in horror before this ontological perversion – something which should not be, yet is."[156]

This is horror fiction that is solely concept-driven, and the next step would be to abandon narrative altogether – or, perhaps, to sublimate narrative into a kind of non-fictional horror. In *Conspiracy*, Ligotti's writing moves from horror fiction to a *concept-horror*.[157] On one page he will engage in a critical examination of a philosophers such as Albert Camus or Miguel de Unamuno, and on the next page his writing will amorphously slide into the prose poetry Ligotti fans will be familiar with: "Then it begins. *This can't be happening,* you think – if you can think at all, if you are anything more than a whirlwind of panic"; "This is the whispering undercurrent that creeps into your thoughts – nothing is safe and nothing is off limits"; "No other life forms know they are alive, and neither do they know they will die. This is our curse alone... Everywhere around us are natural habitats, but within us is the shiver of startling and dreadful things. Simply put: *We are not from here.* If we vanished tomorrow, no organism on this planet would miss us."[158]

It is no surprise that the idea of pessimism lies at the core of *Conspiracy,* and in particular the status of pessimism in an era of radical changes in the environment and global human culture. That idea is encapsulated in what Ligotti calls Zapffe's paradox (named after the philosopher Peter Wessel Zapffe): the height of consciousness is to have revealed the uselessness of consciousness. A variant of this is given by the 19th century German philosopher, poet, and bank clerk Philipp Mainländer, who was deeply influenced by Schopenhauer: "...the knowledge that life is worthless is the flower of all human wisdom."[159] Yet another variant is given in Ligotti's own words: "Nonhuman occupants of this planet are unaware of death. But we are susceptible to startling and dreadful thoughts, and we need some fabulous illusions to take our minds off them."[160] The problem is at once a problem of logic and an existential problem – dare we say, even, a *religious* problem. In Ligotti's exegesis, there is a negativity inherent in everything that exists, from inorganic matter to conscious thought, such that at its most developed state it negates itself (or consumes itself, or fulfills itself). The form of the problem is that, in its most crystalline state, X is tantamount to the negation of X.

Zapffe is an important figure for Ligotti. He not only extends the pessimistic diagnosis of thinkers like Schopenhauer, but he steadfastly refuses any panacea or redemption to the situation. Ligotti summarizes the mountain-climbing philosopher's position: "As Zapffe concluded, we need to hamper our consciousness for all we are worth or it will impose upon us a too clear vision of what we do not want to see, which, as the Norwegian philosopher saw it, along with every other pessimist, is 'the brotherhood of suffering between everything alive.'"[161] In this situation, Zapffe diagnosed the various means that we as human beings have developed for staving off the radically misanthropic tendencies of consciousness (these include strategies such as isolating such thoughts from our everyday lives, anchoring them in belief systems such as religion or science, distracting ourselves with the here and now, and thera-peutic sublimation of such thoughts in artistic expression). Zapffe's conclusions were starkly anti-natalist: not only should we cease from procreating, he suggests, but we should consider the best means by which we as a species can facilitate an extinction that is, in Zapffe's opinion, both inevitable and long overdue.

But Zapffe is only one of many personages that makes an appearance in *Conspiracy*. There is, as one might expect, a discussion of Schopenhauer's thesis that all living beings are blindly driven by an anonymous and indifferent "Will-to-Life." But there is also the German Schopenhauerian and suicide Philipp Mainländer, who suggested a "Will-to-Die" inherent in all beings, living or not – and who speculated on the possibility of God's suicide to correlate with that of human beings. And then there is the Italian writer and philosopher Carlo Michelstaedter, who offers the idea that human beings are the puppets or playthings of unknown forces that may or may not exist – a conspiracy without conspirators. Such thinkers hold a privileged position for Ligotti. Their brand of pessimism refuses any redemptive move towards something beyond pessimism.

Pessimism in this view is not simply a practical form of realism, keeping our feet on the ground and preventing us from getting lost in delusions of grandeur. Pessimism is also not simply another name for secularism, bolstering a renewed faith in human choice and action after the cold shower of the death of God. In short, in Ligotti's hands, pessimism stands in contrast to a "heroic" pessimism that ultimately serves human goals and aspirations (and this comes through in Ligotti's more critical comments on thinkers such as Camus, Unamuno, and contemporary scholars such as Joshua Dienstag and William Brashear).[162]

One of the ideas that best characterizes Ligotti's brand of pessimism is that of the puppet. A leitmotif in much of his work, the puppet is for Ligotti the exemplar of concept-horror, an uncanny manifestation of the life-like that seems to blatantly contradict what we think we know about the world. "We need to know that puppets are puppets," Ligotti notes. "Nevertheless, we may still be alarmed by them. Because if we look at a puppet in a certain way, we may sometimes feel it is looking back, not as a human being looks at us but as a puppet does."[163] Our relationship to an enigmatic, indifferent world in which we are embedded is similar, Ligotti contends, to that of the puppet:

> Human puppets could not conceive of themselves as being puppets at all, not when they are fixed with a consciousness that excites in them the unshakable sense of being singled out from all other objects in creation. Once you begin to feel you are making a go of it on your own – that you are making moves and thinking thoughts which seem to have originated within you – it is not possible for you to believe you are anything but your own master.[164]

This is what intimately ties horror to philosophy – not that philosophy, which explains everything, would explain horror, making it both meaningful and actionable for us, but that philosophy – all philosophy – eventually discovers within itself a hard limit to what can be known, what can be thought, and what can be said. If works of supernatural horror are "philosophical" it is not because they have explained anything – quite the reverse.

And in a sense this also means that what characterizes pessimistic philosophies, particularly the kind that Ligotti is drawn to, is that they have internalized this lesson from the literary tradition of supernatural horror – thinkers like Schopenhauer, Mainländer, or Zapffe unknowingly write philosophy as if they were writers of horror fiction; they make this shift from a philosophy of horror to a horror of philosophy:

> Consciousness is an existential liability, as every pessimist agrees – a blunder of blind nature, according to Zapffe, that has taken humankind down a black hole of logic. To make it through this life, we must make believe that we are not what we are – contradictory beings whose continuance only worsens our plight as mutants who embody the contorted logic of a paradox. To correct this blunder, we should desist from procreating. What could be more judicious or more urgent, existentially speaking, than our self-administered oblivion?[165]

This also means that this kind of thinking, in which horror and philosophy mutually imply each other, must also confront the obvious contradictions that are internal to it. *Conspiracy* is fascinating in this sense because Ligotti is constantly aware of building up a thought that must eventually undermine itself (and this is, no doubt, the reason for the carnivalesque, gallows humor that runs through much of the book). At one moment Ligotti will argue for a relation between the self and the world based on conspiracy – the world as perennially working against us, if only by virtue of the fact that we are mortal beings ephemerally existing in finitude and temporality. But at other moments Ligotti will acknowledge that this too is, in a way, the height of humanist thinking, though a perverted humanism that is still able to conceive of human beings as being the center of the universe (love me, hate me, but let me know that you care...). Here Ligotti will argue for a relation between self and world based on neutrality, indifference, anonymity. And perhaps this is the horror of horrors – the blankness of the world, the blindness of being. Ligotti's thinking constantly wavers between these two aspects of pessimism, between indifference and malignancy, the neutral and the worst.

Conspiracy is a symptom of the pessimist's dilemma: that the worthlessness of life and its philosophical realization tends to become worthwhile (a "no" becomes a "yes"). And in this, *Conspiracy* might be characterized as a form of ecstatic pessimism, a pessimism that is resolutely misanthropic and without redemption, but that also must constantly bear witness to the failure of thought that constitutes it.[166] Yet it is a crumbling of thought that Ligotti has borne witness to again and again. Ligotti's 1994 book *Noctuary* contains a short piece, "The Puppet Masters." It consists of a brief confession of an unnamed narrator who appears to have secret conversations with the puppets, dolls, and marionettes that lay about his room: "Who else would listen to them and express what they have been through? Who else could understand their fears, however petty they may seem at times?" In an uncanny reversal, the narrator begins to suspect he too is a puppet; and the human-like puppets are also alarmingly unhuman. They are mute and indifferent, like puppet masters. The narrator continues, recapping one of Ligotti's recurring motifs, that of the puppet without strings, the conspiracy without conspirators:

Do I ever speak to them of my own life? No; that is, not since a certain incident which occurred some time ago. To this day I don't know what came over me. Absent-mindedly I began confessing some trivial worry, I've completely forgotten what it was. And at that moment all their voices suddenly stopped, every one of them, leaving an insufferable vacuum of silence.[167]

*

Monastery Horror. Literary theorists often talk about "the fantastic" when discussing the horror genre. Tzvetan Todorov, for instance, defines the fantastic as a fork in the road. A character in a story confronts something strange and unexplained, and is presented with one of two options: either the phenomena in question can be explained according to the accepted laws of nature (and it doesn't really exist), or else it cannot be explained (and does exist). Either it's all in your head (and you were dreaming, on drugs, zoning out, had too much coffee, or you're just really imaginative), or else we all have to seriously rethink some basic notions about "reality" (and all those experiments and scientific treatises are for naught). The fantastic is that little moment of hesitation at the fork in the road, a hesitant horror.

Few are the tales that can suspend that duration of uncertainty. (Life, arguably, is different...) In a way, what Lovecraft called "supernatural horror" is such an attempt, and this is exemplified in the tales of contemporary authors such as Laird Barron, Michael Cisco, John Langan, Simon Strantzas, Jeff VanderMeer, and D.P. Watt. Except that what one finds is, with these authors, one expects – looks forward to, even – the fantastic. The hesitation of the fantastic is woven into the very fabric of their story worlds, even though it may at first seem mundane and quotidian. Perhaps there is a categorical imperative embedded within this literary tradition: act as if everything presented to you is *not* what it seems. That forest campsite, a despondent sea-side town, a sluggish rural village, a deserted and ennui-ridden city street, the affectless neutrality of the outskirts of town – these are not just settings for stories but sites of the fantastic, where it "takes place," that ephemeral hesitation given an equal spatial ephemerality. There, all the swirling inter-actions in the world around us become suddenly constricted into solitary and austere estrangements from the world, from the self, from the very language we take for granted. In this suspended moment one finds only an estranged world, an inadequate language, and an uncertain self.

The predecessor for this is that of the monastic tradition. In a way, the monastic cell is the site of the fantastic, stripped to its absolute bare minimum. Although, as the 6th-century *Rule of Benedict* tells us, there are different kinds of monks – cenobites, who live in cloistered communities with other monks, and anchorites or hermits, who live isolated from others – what they have in common is an ongoing practice of stripping away the self through their "spiritual exercise" or *askesis*. Prayer, work, sleep, and contemplation. That is the ideal, at least. What the early monks quickly discovered was that the solitude of the cell and monastery often led to spiritual chaos rather than tranquility. John Cassian, the 4th-century desert monk, described this state as *accedie* – a complicated term that encompasses listlessness, restlessness, torpor, ennui, depression.

Sometimes *accedie* could lead a monk astray, causing them to abandon the practice altogether, or, in other cases, to descend into madness, fever, delusion. Sometimes *accedie* would actually lead to spiritual insights, ambiguous though they could be; *accedie* could itself become a practice, an *askesis*. Guibert of Nogent, an 11th-century Benedictine monk, recounts his struggles with *accedie* in his "Solitary Songs" or *Monodiae* in prose that looks ahead to the gothic tradition:

One night (in winter I believe) I was awakened by an intense feeling of panic. I remained in my bed and felt assured by the light of a lamp close by, which threw off a bright light. Suddenly I heard, not far above me, the clamor of what seemed to me many voices coming out of the dark of night, voices without words. The violence of the clamor struck my temples. I fell unconscious, as if in sleep, and I thought I saw appearing to me a dead man… Terrified by the specter I leapt out of the bed screaming, and as I did so I saw the lamp go out.[168]

A whole tradition of monastery horror could be drawn from this: classics in the gothic literary tradition, such as Matthew Lewis' *The Monk* (1795), modern science fiction classics, such as Fritz Leiber's *Gather, Darkness!* (1950) and Walter M. Miller Jr.'s *A Canticle for Leibowitz* (1959), and late-20th century popular novels such as Umberto Eco's *The Name of the Rose* (1980). One work in particular that captures this sense of monastery horror is Michael Cisco's 1999 novel *The Divinity Student*. Told in a series of short prose sections, it recounts in vivid, florid language the strange death and resurrection of an anonymous protagonist known only as The Divinity Student. Drawn into a network of strange conspiracies, The Divinity Student wanders the desert city of San Veneficio, where he is tasked with compiling the Catalog of Unknown Words, whose true purpose remains enigmatic yet nefarious. From its first passages Cisco's novel refuses any clear distinction between what is "really" happening and what is illusion. Cadavers mingle with lost, old books, and words alchemically seep into the story world with all the solidity of chemical compounds. The result is an uncanny flattening between "it really happened" and "it's all in your head."

Cisco's monastery horror captures the ephemeral and uncertain quality of the fantastic, and, arguably, sustains it through most of the novel. This is largely due to Cisco's language, which is at once lyrical – at times bordering on prose poetry – and yet at the same time fully aware of its inability to capture the fantastic. A poetics of uncertainty, a lyricism of failure. Is this not what many authors in the supernatural horror tradition (most notably, Poe, Lovecraft, Ligotti) secretly aim for?

Ultimately, these examples of monastery horror point back to the source texts of the desert hermits and medieval monks. The place where one hesitates, like a wandering, peripatetic philosopher. Once, a hermit living in the desert of Scetis asked an old hermit there for advice. The old man replied: "Are you still alive? Go and sit in your cell, and think to yourself that you have been in your grave a year already." The hermit returned to his cell, perhaps having learned nothing.

5. As If...

As If. In the 1780s, at the peak of an epoch that ceremoniously referred to itself as "Enlightenment," Immanuel Kant was writing about ethics. Certainly philosophers from Socrates to Spinoza had thought about ethics and morality prior to Kant's time. But during the Enlightenment, which Kant himself would characterize as humanity's coming into "maturity," the stakes were different. If the sleep of reason did indeed produce monsters, it was time for reason to wake up, and to place itself at the center of the quest for knowledge, the pursuit of truth, and the engagement with civil society. In conjunction with paradigm shifts in astronomy, physics, mathematics, and medicine, the so-called human sciences would follow suit, with a new philosophy, a new politics, a new aesthetics, and a new ethics founded exclusively on the authority of human reason, without recourse to religion, myth, or superstition.

But the trick was to develop an ethical and moral philosophy that would go beyond a mere list of "dos" and "don'ts" – a task not only unending but continually subject to change and amendment. In short, Kant was aware that moral and ethical philosophy needed to move beyond mere *hypothetical* imperatives of the type "if A occurs, then do B." Human beings were not, after all, ethical automata, all gears and pulleys cloaked by an anthropomorphic shell. Or were they? Kant's solution was to scale things up, and argue for a morality and ethics that would be unconditional, rather than conditional – what was required was a *categorical* imperative, not just hypothetical imperatives, a "do this" that would apply in each and every case, no matter what the details.

In his 1785 work *Groundwork for the Metaphysics of Morals* Kant provided several definitions of this categorical imperative. One reads: "The categorical imperative would be that which represented an action as objectively necessary of itself, without reference to another end." Another, more thorough definition, reads: "There is, therefore, only a single categorical imperative and it is this: *act only in accordance with that maxim through which you can at the same time will that it become a universal law.*"

The problem, of course, is that it is incredibly difficult to behave in this unconditional manner. It requires an almost *religious* devotion to scientific reason and the cold logic of universal moral law. For every example of such a categorical imperative (e.g. "One should always tell the truth"; "One should always help others") it is easy, all too easy, to think of exceptions, even compounded ones ("…unless telling the truth does not help others…").

And then there is the problem of the "as if." Kant never says that such moral laws *are* universal… or laws… or even moral. What he says is that one should act with such a level of commitment that one would be prepared to claim universal status for such actions. Act *as if* your actions, and the values behind them, are universally valid. Here is another of Kant's definitions of the categorical imperative: "…act *as if* the maxim of your action were to become by your will a universal law of nature."

Just pretend it's for real.

Nevertheless, Kant stood by his categorical imperative, come what may. The implications not only for the individual citizen but for civil society were obvious. The French Revolution, after all, was just around the corner – as was the Terror… phantoms lurking around every moral corner in a labyrinth designed by human beings, for human beings.

*

The Wandering Philosopher. If the age of Enlightenment was about anything, it was about putting theory into practice, about walking the philosophical walk, about showing that reason was not merely an abstract, intellectual exercise with no impact in the "real" world. And Kant loved to walk. Or rather, he walked, without exception, every day, around the town of Königsberg, where he lived for most of his life. Whether he *loved* it or not is another question.

Did the 70-year-old philosopher, while he was writing his ethical treatises, encounter any annoying or difficult people while on his walks? If so, did he view such unfortunate encounters as opportunities to put his "categorical imperative" to the test?

It was often said that the washer-women of Königsberg could tell the time of day by when the elderly but able-bodied Kant walked by their houses.

*

Dethroned. It is often said that the philosophy of Kant effected a "Copernican turn" in the history of thought, just as, a generation earlier, the astronomer Nicolaus Copernicus demonstrated that the sun, and not the earth, was at the center of our planetary system. Even though Copernicus displaced the earth – and by extension humanity – from the center of the universe, he put humanity back in the center by showing how human reason alone – without religion, without scripture, and without the Church – could achieve the *fiat* of scientific explanation.

By the time the industrial dawn of the 20th century came about, scientific reason had explained much – perhaps too much. There was talk of relativity, of the fourth dimension, of the space-time continuum, of elementary particles and the first whisperings of quantum uncertainty. The distance separating the scientific picture of reality and the way reality "ought to be" began to grow further and further apart.

An avid science reader and amateur science journalist, H.P.

171

Lovecraft noted the changes taking place. And they seemed to, once again, displace humanity from the center of the universe. Lovecraft's now-celebrated opening to "The Call of Cthulhu" (published in 1928) summarizes this strange reversal of fortune:

> The most merciful thing in the world, I think, is the inability of the human mind to correlate all its contents. We live on a placid island of ignorance in the midst of black seas of infinity, and it was not meant that we should voyage far. The sciences, each straining in its own direction, have hitherto harmed us little; but some day the piecing together of dissociated knowledge will open up such terrifying vistas of reality, and of our frightful position therein, that we shall either go mad from the revelation or flee from the deadly light into the peace and safety of a new dark age.

Should we then suggest another turn in the Copernican revolution, after Copernicus, and after Kant – a "Lovecraftian turn"? Not only are we human beings not at the center of the universe, we are no longer capable of knowing that we are not at the center of the universe. Our highest cognitive faculties, inclusive of scientific rationality, seem only to lead to paradox, opacity, and, strangely, to mystery. The more we know, the less we know – and what we know of this doesn't bode well for humanity and its self-endowed species superiority.

There is, perhaps, yet another stage after this, closer to our own time. Not much has changed – no one still really understands quantum physics, and everyday reality shows itself to be stranger than fiction. Except that no one cares – or, indeed, bothers to notice. We have become skilled in selectively ignoring the world, even when it shows itself to be blatantly counterintuitive or indifferently non-human. A new *ignorance* is on the horizon, an ignorance borne not of a lack of knowledge but of too much knowledge, too much data, too many theories, too little time.

Strangely, Kant already foresaw this. What he termed the "antinomies of reason" were those issues that could be debated forever and never resolved – the existence of God, the origin of the universe, life after death. Don't bother thinking about these things, he advised, and leave such questions to the theologians or the astronomers – they are not *philosophical* questions.

The humility of philosophy. With Kant, thought becomes humble. With Lovecraft, it also becomes, at the same time, grandiose.

*

Phantasms (III). Where ethical philosophy leaves off, supernatural horror begins. Kant: "...morality is no phantom..."

*

Horror Religiosus. If we accept Lovecraft's genealogy of supernatural horror, we cannot walk away from such works without an acute sense of the senselessness of life – in particular, human life – in its relation to an indifferent cosmos. All the same, human beings populate tales of supernatural horror, and many of them take place within the all-too-familiar confines of human culture. Here we need to briefly return to Todorov's study *The Fantastic*. For Todorov, the hesitation that defines the fantastic is ephemeral. The moment we can rationally explain the fantastic event (e.g. it was just a dream, it was just a bit of visual trickery, it was the fourth dimension, I was on drugs, I am hallucinating) then we leave the fantastic and enter into the uncanny. It only seemed supernatural but can actually be explained (and thus, explained away). However some stories confirm the fantastic as existing outside of our human capabilities of comprehension, and here we again leave the fantastic and enter the domain of the marvelous. It not only seemed but really is supernatural – but then we have to rethink some basic things about what we think we know of the world. Either way, there is a residue of the fantastic that remains unthought, either because it is ignored or because it is not ignored.

If, as per Lovecraft's description, supernatural horror centers on the limit of thought, this limit must also be connected to another limit, the limit of the senses. The failure of thought is tied to the failure of the senses. The aesthetic correlate of the fantastic is what philosophers like Kant called the sublime. Kant's theory of the sublime is well-known. It involves an experience in which I am overwhelmed by my senses, in that they cannot encompass and comprehend what is given to them. This feeling of being overwhelmed is a result of a contrast between my human-scale level of sensing and thinking about the world, and a non-human scale "above" or "below" that of the human scale. For this reason Kant simply defines the sublime as "that which is absolutely great," or conversely, that "in comparison with which all else is small."[169]

Kant's oft-cited, rather gothic examples include: "Bold, overhanging, and, as it were, threatening rocks, thunder-clouds piled up the vault of heaven, borne along with flashes and peals, volcanoes in all their violence of destruction, hurricanes leaving desolation in their track, and boundless ocean rising with rebellious force, the high waterfall of some mighty river, and the like, make our power of resistance of trifling moment in comparison with their might."[170] In the sublime, the human is humbled, even humiliated, a mere speck in contrast to something impersonal, vast, and indifferent. The sublime "forces upon us the recognition of our physical helplessness as beings of nature," the strange allure of our own insignificance, "astonishment amounting almost to terror."[171]

At the same time that my senses are overwhelmed, I am experiencing something, and what I am experiencing is my senses being overwhelmed. What I "sense" is the failure of the senses. At the limit of the human being's capacity for sensing and thinking is the sense of the limit of the senses, and likewise, the thought of the limit of thought. "Thus, too, delight in the sublime in nature is only *negative*... that is to say it is a feeling of imagination by its own act depriving itself of its freedom..."[172]

This is where, for Kant, the sublime turns from tragic to heroic. For it is precisely in this awareness of limits that the human being redeems itself. It is in this awareness, which is not itself sensory – a "supersensible substrate" – that we are able to think these limits, including the limit of thought. As Kant notes, "the mere ability even to think the given infinite without contradiction, is something that requires the presence in the human mind of a faculty that is itself supersensible."[173]

I've always found Kant's heroic, humanist recuperation of the sublime disappointing. It is not necessarily wrong, just disappointing. Must the human being conquer the world into which it's thrown, even at the moment of its being overwhelmed and rendered insignificant? Must the failure automatically turn into a success? The tricky part lies in the dilemma Kant points to: the human being at once determined by its limits and thinking beyond its limits. It is perhaps for this reason that Kant repeated describes the sublime in ambiguous, contradictory terms: as a "delightful horror," or alternately, a "tranquility tinged with terror."[174]

These ambiguous affects suggest that the sublime has a relation to certain kinds of religious experience. No doubt this is why theologian Rudolf Otto uses the Latin phrase *mysterium tremendum* to describe what he calls "the holy." But for Otto the holy has nothing to do with the moral and religious connotations it often has. The holy is not good, and neither is it good "for us" as human beings. Central to this is what Otto refers to as the "creature-feeling," akin to Kant's description of the sublime rendering the human insignificant. Humbled before what is vaster and slower than entire empires, the human being can only register a negative awareness, and this is, for Otto, the core of religious phenomena: "The truly 'mysterious' object is beyond our apprehension and comprehension, not only because our knowledge has certain irremovable limits, but because in it we come upon something inherently 'wholly other,' whose kind and character are incommensurable with our own, and before which we therefore recoil in a wonder that strikes us chill and numb."[175] Otto uses the term *numinous* to describe this shadowy, excessive, non-human aspect of the holy, an experience of the "wholly other" that can only be described as a negative experience.

Otto's study takes up the sublime and suggests a link to religious phenomena. Literary historians and critics would suggest a further link to the horror genre. As religious authority was in crisis, and scientific rationality on the rise, the Enlightenment gave birth to cultural forms that expressed both a suspicion regarding traditional religion and at the same time an ambiguous desire for religious experience. Devendra Varma's study *The Gothic Flame*, which deals primarily with the gothic novel, puts it plainly: "...the Gothic novels arose out of a quest for the numinous."[176] He continues, noting that "these novels indicate a new, tentative apprehension of the Divine... The ghosts and demons, the grotesque manifestations of the supernatural, aroused the emotions by which man had first discovered his soul and realized the presence of a Being greater far than he, one who created and destroyed at will."[177]

In his book *Haunted Presence*, S.L. Varnado is even more explicit, noting that "Otto's concept of the numinous provides insights into the spirit of Gothic and supernatural horror."[178] The stock-and-trade of gothic fiction – "mountain gloom, lonely castles, phantom ships, violent storms, and the vastness of sea and polar regions... magical lore, apparitions, ghouls, vampires, or revenants" – are echoed in Otto's own evocations of "darkness," "silence," and "vast and empty distances" as emblems of the numinous. They are also found in Kant's description of the sublime. Varnado also highlights the duplicity of the numinous – at once a subjective affect, and yet also the failure of subjectivity as it confronts something radically non-human, something "wholly other," that registers itself as the failure to have an experience at all.

This failure is where horror and religion meet. Instead of the more clichéd images of ebullient, overflowing, radiant experiences of fullness and light, these phenomena – the sublime, the numinous, the gothic – are instead failures of experience, and therefore, failures of the human sensory and cognitive apparatus. It is the difference between an experience of horror and a horrific experience, the latter annulling any possibility of experience whatsoever. Thus one finds, in mystics such as Meister Eckhart, John of the Cross, and in the anonymous *Cloud of Unknowing*, self-annulling descriptions of the divine in terms of darkness, nothingness, an abyss, a desert, a dark night – descriptions that are as much about the "negativity of experience" as they are about "experiences of negation."[179] Writing about medieval Christian mysticism, Denys Turner clarifies this distinction, noting that "there is a very great difference between the strategy of *negative propositions* and the strategy of *negating the propositional*; between that of the *negative image* and that of the *negation of imagery*."[180]

What remains of the sublime but this residue of the human being, not so long ago confident in its capacity for apprehending and comprehending the world around it as the world in its own image? What remains but a sublime of indifference, anonymity, impersonality – an impersonal sublime?[181]

*

A Once-Living Shadow. The terms phantasmagoria, phantasm, and phantom all share a common etymological root, from the

Greek *phantazein* (to make visible) and *phainein* (to show). Strange, then, that the terms would come to denote precisely that which is not seen, or rather, that which is seen with uncertainty. The tradition of the gothic novel is replete with phantoms of this type; we as readers are never sure if the characters have actually seen a ghost or have simply mis-judged the night wind languorously blowing a curtain.

But every phantom – real or imagined – is doubled, referring to a once-living person as well as being a spectral manifestation in and of itself. Every phantom is literally beside itself, not unlike the many disenchanted characters in the stories of *The Phantasmagorical Imperative*... "to be besides oneself" – as one's own shadow, as a doppelgänger, as one who exists twice... perhaps twice more than necessary.

*

Phantasms (IV). The phantasmagorical imperative: everything unreal must appear. The phantom imperative: act as if everything real is unreal.

*

The World Becomes a Phantom. Kant's philosophy is, to be sure, philosophy in the grand style – rigorous, systematic, ambitious... and a touch naive. For, how many of us are really capable of acting according to the cold logic of reason, irrespective of our individual desires, our displaced egos, our fears and tremblings?

Kant seemed aware of this. Near the end of one of his treatises he admits, almost confessionally: "Now, such a kingdom of ends would actually come into existence through maxims whose rule the categorical imperative prescribes to all rational beings *if they were universally followed*." The stakes are too high, it seems. It only works if *everyone* plays along.

But the truly disturbing thing is not just that other people might not act accordingly, but that the whole non-human world may not act accordingly – *that the world itself may not play along*. Objects behaving strangely, familiar places suddenly unfamiliar, the inorganic world suddenly staring back. Kant continues: "It is true that, even though a rational being scrupulously follows this maxim himself, he cannot for that reason count upon every other to be faithful to the same maxim nor can he count upon the kingdom of nature and its purposive order to harmonize with him, as a fitting member, toward a kingdom of ends possible through himself, that is, upon its favoring his expectation of happiness..."

*

Spectral Suicide. In the 17th century the philosopher, occultist, and scientist Athanasius Kircher designed a novel device using a simple candle-powered magic lantern and glass slide. A product of Kircher's interests in optics, he also associated these so-called phantasmagoria and their ability to produce lifelike, animate images with a kind of vitalistic life-force. Such devices proliferated across the cultural centers of 18th and 19th century Europe, including the Parisian Cabaret du Néant, where visitors could enjoy a ghost show along with their absinthe. Soon magic lantern shows and phantasmagoria could be seen everywhere, along with stereoscopes and other visual media – much of which could be purchased in the then-popular Parisian arcades, with their rows of magical shop window displays – uncanny mannequins, dismembered hats, shoes, gloves, necklaces, walking canes, eyeglasses, children's toys ...the various charms of an era quickly disappearing. It was no wonder that Walter Benjamin, living in Paris in the 1920s, would describe the modern commodities of European cities as so many phantasmagoria.

Predominately used for entertainment purposes, the

enchanting qualities of 18th and 19th-century phantasmagoria were also taken quite seriously by those interested in magic and the occult. In Leipzig, the inventor, coffee-shop owner, and occultist Johann Schröpfer designed his own phantasmagoria, which he shared with his Freemason colleagues. Schröpfer would himself become a phantasmagoria. So taken was he by its conjuring powers and life-like qualities of its spectral images, that, during one demonstration, Schröpfer claimed that a dead person could be resurrected through its powers. It is said that, in or around 1774, Schröpfer attempted to prove his theories by killing himself on stage. The subsequent revitalization was not, however, successful.

*

An Argument for the Categorical Imperative. "I haven't read as many books as you have, but if they make you this miserable I don't think I want to."

*

Hymn to Horror. "All concepts and with them all principles are nevertheless related to empirical intuitions, i.e., to data for possible experience. Without this they have no objective validity at all, but are rather a mere play, whether it be with representations of the imagination or of the understanding."[182]

Philosophers such as Kant tell us that our senses are like glasses we can never take off. If philosophy is a form of conjuring, then what of physics, which speaks to us cryptically of waves, particles, and strings? Both use reason to reveal to us the most unreasonable of propositions – that the world is not "our" world, but a world bereft of humanity, a world that impassively tolerates the ostentatious stage that we have placed at its center, with us stage center, performing endless soliloquies of impermanence. If philosophy is a form of magic, then physics is a necromancy. Perhaps poetry goes even further – a hymn.

*

Unholy Matter. In the town of Siena, in the Basilica San Domenico, resides the head of Saint Catherine of Siena, a 14th century mystic and theologian, who was also active in the religious politics of her time. The head of Catherine – sometimes referred to as the "Holy Head" or "Sacred Head" – is contained in an ornate silver shrine in the form of a miniature gothic temple. Long said to have miraculous powers, the head of Catherine was originally brought to the Basilica by Raymond of Capua, a Dominic monk who was both Catherine's confessor and her hagiographer. After Catherine's death, there was some dispute about where her remains should reside, whether in Rome, the seat of the Church and the place where Catherine had died, or in Siena, her hometown. According to one oft-repeated account, Raymond, attempting to bring Catherine's body back to Siena, realized that the Church authorities would never allow this. Instead, he detached her head from her body, and, placing it in a sack, carried it out of Rome. But he was stopped by the guards. When they looked in the sack, they saw it was filled with roses. They returned the sack to Raymond and sent him on his way back to Siena, where, it is said, Catherine's severed head rematerialized from the sack of roses.

The head of Catherine is one of many relics of Christian saints preserved to this day. The list of relics within Christianity alone is long and varied. It includes the hand of Teresa of Avila, the arm of Mary Magdalene, and the Shroud of Turin, a cloth on which Jesus is said to have dried his face, and which contains his image. After the death of Claire of Assisi, it is reported that guards had to be stationed around her body, as followers thronged towards the corpse, attempting to take away bits and pieces of it. When the corpse of Anthony of Padua was discovered to have incorruptible parts – the tongue, jaw, left arm and hand – were detached from the rest of the corpse and encased in separate reliquaries. Specially-constructed vessels were created for such relics, often with ornate designs custom shaped to the body part in question. Tombs long-hidden from plain sight were unearthed and put on display, the corpses in crypts visible through viewing windows on the floor.

Although the veneration of relics in Christianity began as early as the 3rd century, the practice grew in the later Middle Ages. Though perhaps strange to the modern, secular mind, the theories and practices surrounding relics open onto more general questions concerning our embodied, material existence as human beings – and the limits of our ability to fully comprehend that materiality. As medieval historian Caroline Walker Bynum notes:

> The transformed statues, chalices, wafers, cloths, relics, and even mounds of earth to which the faithful made pilgrimage in the fourteenth and fifteenth centuries presented a challenge that was theoretical as well as practical for a religion that held that the entire material world was created by and could therefore manifest God...Issues of how matter behaved, both ordinarily and miraculously, when in contact with an infinitely powerful and ultimately unknowable God were key to devotion and theology.[183]

The holy matter Bynum studies includes "animated statues; bleeding hosts, walls, and images; holy dust or cloth that itself mediated further transformation"[184] in addition to traditional relics (body parts or bones of saints), effluvial relics (material that miraculously secreted or oozed from the bodies of saints or from holy objects), sacramental objects (including the Eucharist), as well as animistic devotional images such as prayer cards and winged altarpieces.

For Bynum, "there was a basic understanding of matter that underlay both medieval practices and the complicated, learned arguments that concerned relics, images, sacramentals, and *Dauerwunder*." Such instances of holy matter were as much about practice as they were about theory; indeed, in many of the instances of Bynum studies, the devotional practices surrounding holy matter takes precedence over the abstract theological discussions of them. What holy matter reveals is a premodern understanding of materiality that is also, in a way, remarkably contemporary: "In contrast to the modern tendency to draw sharp distinctions between animal, vegetable, and mineral, or between animate and inanimate, the natural philosophers of the Middle Ages understood matter as the locus of generation and corruption."[185] Hence, for the cluster of discourses surrounding holy matter, "the basic way of describing matter... was to see it as organic, fertile, and in some sense alive."[186]

Matter is unstable, unpredictable, innovative, ambivalent – especially when the matter is the stuff of our own bodies, often obeying an occult logic of its own, continuing to live bit by bit, continuing to die bit by bit. Perhaps the various "miracles" that populate supernatural horror are, in a way, variations of holy matter. Except that the world of supernatural horror stories is a secular world, where no one believes, at least not without empirical "proof." And yet there occur in the normal, day-to-day world irruptions of paradoxical matter: from the living dead to the undead, from human-animal metamorphoses to creatures that have no name, from resurrected bodies to autonomous body parts, from ominous and animate objects to accursed secret books, from the atheistic passion plays of "splatterhorror" to the mesmerizing dissipations of "cosmic horror." Matter behaving indifferently to the self-conscious human beings that it composes and decomposes. An unholy matter...

Of the Sacred Head, enshrined in its uncannily preserved,

gothic splendor, Raymond of Capua remarks: "she began to build up in her mind a secret cell which she vowed she would never leave for anything in the world."[187]

*

Qualitas Occulta. We can make a list, a partial list (it will always be partial). There is the *Book of Azathoth*, the *Book of Eibon*, the *Cthäat Aquadingen*, the *Cultes des Ghoules*, *De Masticatione Mortuorum in Tumulis*, *De Vermis Mysteriis*, the *Liber Ivonis*, the *Revelations of Glaaki*, the *Unaussprechlichen Kulten*, the Pnakotic Manuscripts, the Sigsand Manuscripts, the G'harne Fragments, the Poakotic Fragments, and then there is, of course, the *Necronomicon*. This is but a short sampling. All real books, all existent within the often inter-connected stories of authors such as William Hope Hodgson, Robert Chambers, H.P. Lovecraft, Clark Ashton Smith, Frank Belknap Long, Robert E. Howard, August Derleth, Brian Lumley, Robert Bloch, Lin Carter, Ramsey Campbell, T.E.D. Klein, Thomas Ligotti, and possibly uncountable others.

They are penned by obscure and neglected authors, most of whom have gone mad or mysteriously disappeared. The books themselves are difficult to find; if one is lucky there is a dusty old copy in the Miskatonic University library (though you will most likely find it has mysteriously gone missing). One almost never mentions them casually (as in "What are you reading?" "Oh, just the *Necromonicon*"). They are mentioned – when they are mentioned – with ominous ceremony. The dreaded *Necronomicon*, the unmentionable *Book of Eibon*, the blasphemous *De Vermis Mysteriis*.

The idea that a person might be driven mad by a book is fantastical, even absurd – especially today, as books themselves seem to be vanishing into an ether of oblique references. We are so used to the idea of consuming books for the information they contain that we rarely consider the possibility that the books might in turn consume us. Thomas Frognall Dibdin's *The Bibliomania; or, Book-Madness* (1809) uses a quasi-medical diagnosis to describe individuals literally consumed by books, obsessed not just with their contents, but with their materiality: "There is, first, a passion for Large Paper Copies; secondly, for Uncut Copies; thirdly, for Illustrated Copies; fourthly, for Unique Copies; fifthly, for Copies printed upon Vellum; sixthly, for First Editions; seventhly, for True Editions; and eighthly, for Books printed in the Black-Letter."[188]

Holbrook Jackson's *Anatomy of Bibliomania* (1930) goes further, tracing that fine line where the love of books (bibliophilia) turns into its dark other of book madness (bibliomania). The madness of possessing books turns with great subtlety into the madness of being possessed by books. Jackson even recounts what is no doubt the pinnacle of bibliomania – the "bibliophages," who are so consumed by their books that they eat them, incorporating them into their anatomies, effacing all distinction between the literal and the figurative, perhaps resulting in an unnamable, material "thing" not unlike that which populates the dimly-read pages of these forbidden books.

The somber and sorrowful *Songs from the Black Moon* of Rasu-Yong Tugen, Baroness de Tristeombre. The frenetic, stigmatic *Cantos for the Crestfallen* of Pseudo-Leopardi, only recently discovered. Pir Iqbal the Impaled's curious tomes of visceral and geometric "flagellant hymns." The still black waters that course through Bonaventura's *Die Nachtwachen*...

*

Phantasms (V). ...fragile and numinous, tentacles longer than night...

Notes

Portions of this book have previously appeared in the following publications: *And They Were Two In One and One In Two* (eds. Nicola Masciandaro and Eugene Thacker); *Angelaki*; *Beyond Biopolitics* (eds. Patricia Clough and Craig Willse); Clive Barker, *Cabal and Other Annotations* (ed. Jason Cook); *Collapse*; D.P. Watt, *The Phantasmagorical Imperative*; *Incognetum Hactenus*; *Leper Creativity* (eds. Ed Keller, Nicola Masciandaro, and Eugene Thacker); *Mute*; *Terence Hannum – Veils*; and at lectures given at the CUNY Graduate Center, Johns Hopkins University, The New School, SUNY-Stony Brook/AC Institute, and the University of Naples. My gratitude to those involved in organizing these publications and events. Special thanks to the crew at Zero Books. Thanks also to AR, AS, ELT, JA, MST, MT, NM, RB, SC, TG, TL, and PM.

1. Edgar Allan Poe, "The Black Cat," in *The Portable Edgar Allan Poe*, ed. J. Gerald Kennedy (New York: Penguin, 2006), p. 192.
2. H.P. Lovecraft, "The Shadow Out of Time," in *The Dreams in the Witch House and Other Weird Stories*, ed. S.T. Joshi (New York: Penguin, 2004), p. 335.
3. This is detailed in Lovecraft's long essay *Supernatural Horror in Literature* (ed. S.T. Joshi, Hippocampus Press, 2000), in which supernatural horror is defined in relation to the fear of the unknown. In his essay Lovecraft assembles a genealogy of horror literature that is still valuable to this day.
4. Tzvetan Todorov, *The Fantastic: A Structural Approach to a Literary Genre*, trans. Richard Howard (Ithaca: Cornell University Press, 1975), p. 25. There is a significant body of critical work on Todorov's notion of the fantastic, such as

Noël Carroll's *Philosophy of Horror*, Rosemary Jackson's *Fantasy: The Literature of Subversion*, Farah Mendlesohn's *Rhetorics of Fantasy*, Eric Rabkin's *The Fantastic in Literature*, as well as the literary criticism of Istvan Csicsery-Ronay Jr. (especially his book *The Seven Beauties of Science Fiction*) and weird fiction scholar S.T. Joshi (especially his books *The Weird Tale* and *The Modern Weird Tale*). An older collection, *Literature of the Occult* (ed. Peter Messent), is still relevant.

5. Ibid.

6. Cited in the Introduction to Dante, *The Divine Comedy – Volume I: Inferno*, trans. Mark Musa (New York: Penguin, 2003), p. 42. Dante continues, using a Biblical quote as example: "So that this method of exposition may be clearer, one may consider it in these lines: 'When Israel came out of Egypt, the house of Jacob from people of strange language, Judah was his sanctuary and Israel his dominion.' If we look only at the letter, this signifies that the children of Israel went out of Egypt in the time of Moses; if we look at the allegory, it signifies our redemption through Christ; if we look at the moral sense, it signifies the turning of the souls from the sorrow and misery of sin to a state of grace; if we look at the anagogical sense, it signifies the passage of the blessed souls from the slavery of this corruption to the freedom of eternal glory." Dante also discusses allegory in a work of literary criticism known as the *Convivio* (*The Banquet*).

7. Dante, *The Letters of Dante*, ed. and trans. Paget Toynbee (Oxford: Clarendon Press, 1966), pp. 199-200.

8. Dante, *The Divine Comedy, Volume 1: Inferno*, trans. Mark Musa (New York: Penguin, 1984), III.9, p. 89.

9. I limit myself to a consideration of diagrams of Dante's Hell as a whole. There is, of course, a whole tradition of art based on individual scenes from the *Inferno*, from Botticelli to Gustav Doré to Salvador Dalí and contemporary artists

such as Wayne Barlowe.

10. There does exist a video game called *Dante's Inferno*, produced by EA and released in 2010. It is, however, nothing more than a first-person shooter, and a disappointing adaptation of Dante's text. There was also a *Dante's Inferno* game made for the Commodore 64 and released in 1986.

11. Aristotle, in the *Nicomachean Ethics*, Book VII, divides wrongful behavior into the three rough categories of uncontrolled appetite, perversions of appetites, and the deceitful use of appetites.

12. Hobbes, *Leviathan: With Selected Variants from the Latin Edition of 1668*, ed. Edwin Curley (Indianapolis: Hackett, 1994), "Introduction."

13. Plato, *Republic*, trans. Desmond Lee (New York: Penguin, 2003), IV.444a-e, p. 154.

14. Paul, *I Corinthians* 12: 12-31, New International Version. The text continues: "As it is, there are many parts, but one body. The eye cannot say to the hand, 'I don't need you!' And the head cannot say to the feet, 'I don't need you!' On the contrary, those parts of the body that seem to be weaker are indispensable, and the parts that we think are less honorable we treat with special honor."

15. Gilson, *The Spirit of Medieval Philosophy*, trans. A.H.C. Downes (Notre Dame: University of Notre Dame Press, 1991), p. 171.

16. Kantorowicz, *The King's Two Bodies: A Study in Medieval Political Theology* (Princeton: Princeton University Press, 1997), p. 231.

17. Le Goff, "Head or Heart? The Political Use of Body Metaphors in the Middle Ages," trans. Patricia Ranum, *Fragments for a History of the Human Body, Vol. III*, eds. Michel Feher, Ramona Naddaff and Nadia Tazi (New York: Zone, 1989), p. 22.

18. Cf., for instance, Book XVIII of Augustine's *De Civitate dei*, and

chapters 1-3 of Aquinas, *De Regimine Principum*.

19. Taubes summarizes the basic positions of such debates: the solution of representation (in which a single secular ruler is God's representative on earth), the solution of dual sovereignty (in which a strict division between spiritual and temporal authority is posited), and the solution of theocracy (in which the Church obtains sovereignty, unmediated by secular or temporal powers).

20. Schmitt, *Political Theology: Four Chapters on the Concept of Sovereignty*, trans. Tracy Strong, ed. George Schwab (Chicago: University of Chicago Press, 2006), p. 36.

21. Taubes, *The Political Theology of Paul*, trans. Dana Hollander, ed. Aleida Assman and Jan Assman (Stanford: Stanford University Press, 2004), p. 142.

22. Gierke, *Natural Law and the Theory of Society, 1500-1800*, trans. Ernest Barker (Clark, NJ: Lawbook Exchange Ltd., 2002), p. 42.

23. Ibid.

24. See, for instance Ockham's "A Dialogue" III.I.2, in *A Letter to the Friars Minor and Other Writings*, ed. Arthur Stephen McGrade and John Kilcullen, trans. John Kilcullen, (Cambridge: Cambridge University Press 1995).

25. Hobbes, *Leviathan*, Part II, Chapter XXIX, "Of those things that Weaken, or tend to the Dissolution of a Commonwealth."

26. Plato, *Republic*, VIII, 556e, p. 235.

27. Nicholas of Cusa, *The Catholic Concordance (De Concordantia Catholica)*, trans. Paul Sigmund (Cambridge: Cambridge University Press, 1996 [1431-33]), III, XLI, p. 593.

28. The scholarly work of Ed Cohen, Sander Gilman, Emily Martin, and Laura Otis stand out in this regard.

29. A similar dynamic is at work in the early 21st century, if, as it is said, terrorism is the "autoimmune" condition of politics. Jacques Derrida's comments on the "autoimmu-

nitary" condition of security appear in Giovanna Borradori, *Philosophy in a Time of Terror: Dialogues with Jürgen Habermas and Jacques Derrida* (Chicago: University of Chicago Press, 2003).

30. The concept of the "necro" has also been theorized by Nick Land, *The Thirst for Annihilation* (London: Routledge, 1992), Reza Negarastani, "Death as Perversion: Openness and Germinal Death," *Ctheory* (15 October 2003), www.ctheory.net, as well as in Achille Mbembe's essay "Necropolitics," *Public Culture* 15.1 (2003): 11-40. My use of the concept here is derived not from contemporary theory but from a literary lineage: the tradition from the graveyard poets and the 18th-century gothic novel to plague fictions, which range quite broadly from Boccaccio, to Defoe, to Mary Shelley's underrated *The Last Man*, to Albert Camus and Octavia Butler.

31. In fact, one could, albeit heuristically, re-organize political theory along the axis of plague, pestilence, and epidemics. The ancient body politic (represented by Plato's anatomization and Aristotle's animism) would have to be considered within the context of the Plague of Athens (431 BCE), and the siege on Athens during the Peloponnesian War. The late-Medieval body politic (represented by its foundations in Paul and Augustine, and its formalization by Aquinas) would have to be considered alongside the recurrent outbreaks of bubonic plague during the 13th and 14th centuries (of which the Black Death of 1347-51 is the most devastating instance), as well as the subsequent social disorder and long-term restructuring of property relations that it entailed. Finally, the modern body politic (represented by natural right theory) would have to be considered against the Great Plague of London (1665), which took place in the midst of civil war and renewed debates about secular sovereignty. From a contemporary vantage point, they also

have the following commonalities: A combination of political theory, civil strife or war, and an outbreak of a disease; the ambivalent role of networks of communication, travel, and trade as at once constituting the body politic and dissolving it; these are coupled with a range of political and theological responses to what is identified as a state of emergency; and the result that, in these instances, a thinking about the body politic's figural "diseases" becomes inseparable from the actual diseases that spread through a population.

32. This is presented in the first few lectures of *Security, Territory, Population. Lectures at the Collège de France, 1977-1978*, ed. Michael Senellart, trans. Graham Burchell (New York: Palgrave Macmillan, 2007). It is worth noting that the English term "security" often covers two French terms: *sûreté*, which refers more to "national security," or the security afforded by military forces (to secure internal or external threats), and *sécurité*, which refers to the management of risk in such instances as social security or health insurance. On the surface, the two French terms appear to split into foreign (*sûreté*) and domestic security (*sécurité*). However activities such as public health surveillance or the governmental management of an epidemic are examples that frustrate this neat division.

33. Ibid., p. 64.

34. Ibid., p. 23.

35. Ibid., p. 46.

36. In this case, multiplicity is not the Platonic dialectic of the "one" and the "many" (in which the "one" always wins), and neither is it a Deleuzian-Bergsonian multiplicity, that posits an organization outside of the One-many relationship altogether.

37. The issue, then, is not simply Aristotelian-Thomist "animation" but rather Lovecraftian "re-animation."

38. Dante, *Inferno*, Canto IX, 104-129. Italian consulted at the Digital Dante Project, dante.ilt.columbia.edu.

39. They include the Epicureans, who question the immortality of the soul, but also members of the warring Guelf and Ghibelline parties of Dante's own time.

40. But what is striking is that Dante can only express this by, in effect, turning the body politic upside-down, in which it seems to function even more efficiently than in the more vague topologies of *Purgatario*'s penitentiary-like cliffs, or the abstract, celestial geometry of *Paradiso*...

41. This combination – a sovereign-medical intervention in death, and the context of colonialism – has meant that, in such films, the living dead are often an amalgam of the colonized population and slave labor. In this regard many of Fulci's films are explicit references to *The Island of Doctor Moreau*. At the end of *Zombie*, for instance, the living dead rise and begin to move in their massing form from the isolated context of the colonial island to – gasp – "civilization."

42. Maurice Blanchot, *The Writing of the Disaster*, trans. Ann Smock (Lincoln: University of Nebraska Press, 1995), p. 1.

43. Hypothetically, public health concerns in the U.S. are more or less separated from military concerns: the CDC (Centers for Disease, Control, and Prevention) specializes in the former, while branches of the military such as USAMRIID (United States Army Medical Research Institute for Infectious Disease) specialize in public health directly related to biological and chemical warfare. The reality, of course, is more complicated; in the U.S., the term "biodefense" has exponentially widened to include both bioterrorist attacks as well as a whole new category of "emerging infectious diseases."

44. In the U.S., the flurry of biodefense policies developed after 9/11 have arguably shifted the conceptual base of previous

public health initiatives. I can note, in passing, a few of them: the Bioterrorism Act ("Public Health Security and Bioterrorism Preparedness and Response Act of 2002"), which involves the regulation and monitoring of materials such as food, livestock, microbes by multiple agencies; Project BioShield (also 2002), which mobilizes research in the pharmaceutical sector towards the production of "medical countermeasures," a "national pharmaceutical stockpile," and a new FDA "fast-track" approval process for vaccines; the Biosurveillance Program (2003), which takes up medical surveillance initiatives at the CDC from the 1990s (e.g. BioWatch, the National Electronic Disease Surveillance System) and aims for a real-time, nation-wide, medical surveillance system. Developments such as these have in part contributed to the influx of federal funds for biodefense research, and all of this has taken place alongside ongoing investigations into the U.S. military's classified bioweapons research, which include, among other purported programs, the construction of ad-hoc germ weapons labs and the engineering of weapons-grade, antibiotic-resistant anthrax. Ongoing global concerns over flu pandemics have prompted the U.S. Office of Health and Human Services, in their "Pandemic Influenza Strategic Plan" of 2005, to devise hypothetical doomsday scenarios.

45. Isidore Ducasse, Comte de Lautréamont, *Maldoror: The Complete Works of the Comte de Lautréamont*, trans. Alexis Lykiard (Cambridge: Exact Change, 1994), pp. 101-102.

46. Ibid., pp. 131-32.

47. Ibid., p. 276. The review was published in *La Jeunesse* 5 (Sept. 1868).

48. Antonin Artaud, "Letter on Lautréamont," *Artaud Anthology*, trans. Jack Hirschman (San Francisco: City Lights, 1965), p. 125.

49. Mario Praz, *The Romantic Agony*, trans. Angus Davidson

(New York: Meridian, 1963), p. 163.

50. *Maldoror*, p. 258. From a letter to Poulet-Malassis, 23 Oct. 1869.

51. Peter Nesselroth, *Lautréamont's Imagery: A Stylistic Approach* (Paris: Droz, 1969), p. 69. This is also the approach adopted by works associated with the journal *Tel Quel*, the most notable example of which is Julia Kristeva's *Revolution in Poetic Language*.

52. Alex de Jonge, *Nightmare Culture: Lautréamont and "Les Chants de Maldoror"* (New York: St. Martin's, 1973), p. 82.

53. Ibid., p. 84.

54. Alain Paris, "Le Bestiare des Chants de Maldoror," in *Quatre Lectures de Lautréamont* (Paris: Nizet, 1972), p. 6, translation mine.

55. Gaston Bachelard, *Lautréamont*, trans. James Hillman and Robert S. Dupree (Dallas: Dallas Institute, 1986), p. 2.

56. Ibid., p. 3.

57. Ibid., p. 79.

58. Ibid., p. 3. Bachelard also goes on to contrast *Maldoror* to Kafka's "Metamorphosis," Kipling's *The Jungle Book*, and Wells's *The Island of Dr. Moreau*.

59. Ibid., p. 16.

60. Ibid., p. 60.

61. Ibid., p. 27.

62. Lautréamont is not the first to suggest this intersection – arguably it can be found in early modern bestiaries and teratologies, where the language of science and fable intermingle. More importantly, it is a point taken up in the contemporary theory, in Deleuze and Guattari's discussion of animality in *Kafka*, and in Akira Lippit's notion of "animetaphor," developed in his book *Electric Animal*.

63. Bachelard, *Lautréamont*, p. 84.

64. Aristotle, *On the Soul/Parva Naturalia/On Breath*, trans. W.S. Hett (Cambridge, MA: Harvard UP/Loeb Classical Library,

2000), p. 69.

65.   Ibid.

66.   Bachelard, *Lautréamont*, p. 83.

67.   Ibid., p. 6.

68.   Liliane Durand-Dessert, *La Guerre Sainte: Lautréamont et Isidore Ducasse* (Nancy: Presses Universitaires de Nancy, 1991), p. 3, translation mine.

69.   Bachelard, *Lautréamont*, p. 86. The weakest part of analyses such as Bachelard's – and his is not the only study of *Maldoror* to fall into this trap – is his refusal to fully accept the stark antihumanism that courses through *Maldoror*. Ultimately, for Bachelard the animality of *Maldoror* comes to be regarded as a testament to a kind of super-human capacity for imagination and the poetics of form – even at the moment when the text so violently revolts against the human. For Bachelard the animality of *Maldoror* is really about *poiesis*, the creation of new forms, what Bachelard terms a "poetry of the project" or simply the "open imagination." The successive, incessant, and aggressive transformations in *Maldoror* come to be seen as an indicator of the human passing beyond the animal, and finally passing beyond itself. Bachelard again: "At that point, man appears as the sum of vital possibilities, as a *super-animal*. All of animality is at his disposal" (p. 11). Indeed, many of the classic studies of *Maldoror* want to recuperate this antihumanism into a renewed, romantic humanism that valorizes vague, human-specific capacities such as the "poetic imagination" or the like. While we may agree with Bachelard's attempts to move animality beyond "the animal," it remains unclear how such a "firmly deanimalized thought" avoids simply re-instating the human at the top of the pyramid. And, even if we take Bachelard to mean "imagination" in a broadly non-human sense, it is unclear why an explicitly poetic text, belonging explicitly to human culture, would be

the avatar of this open imagination. Why not, for instance, make the claim that the generative metamorphoses and morphologies of nature itself are the true exemplars of the open imagination? For a text that so virulently poises itself against humanity, it would seem strange to hold up *Maldoror* as the pinnacle of imaginative achievement, human or otherwise. For much of *Maldoror* scholarship, antihumanism and animality co-exist in an uneasy relationship. Antihumanism ultimately leads to a renewed humanism of the imagination, an elevation once again of the human above the animal. Hence animality is subsumed within humanity (though a humanity of imagination rather than reason). Such as view of *Maldoror* is really, then, a poetic *sacrifice* of animality for a renewed humanity.

70. Pseudo-Dionysius (Dionysius the Areopagite), *The Complete Works*, trans. Paul Rorem (New York: Paulist, 1988), p. 138.

71. Although the term anamorphosis has a double meaning – in art history to describe a visual illusion, and in biology to describe the development of embryonic life forms – I am using the term to describe a breaking-down of form and the forming capacity. Thus *ana-morphosis* is, in this case, a literal layering of negative form (*ana-* "back," "reversion," "again") on top of existing form (*morphē*, "shape," "form").

72. Lautréamont, *Maldoror*, pp. 142-43.

73. Ibid., pp. 159-60.

74. The appropriation of this passage is pointed out in a still-useful 1952 article by Maurice Viroux, "Lautréamont et le Dr. Chenu" (published in the *Mercure de France*), where Viroux traces it to an almost verbatim passage in the volume *Oiseaux* of Chenu's *Encyclopédie*.

75. Paris, "Le Bestiare," pp. 115-16; translation mine.

76. Bachelard, *Lautréamont*, p. 90.

77. François Laruelle, "A Summary of Non-philosophy" trans. Ray Brassier, *Pli: The Warwick Journal of Philosophy* 8 (1999),

p. 139.

78. Gilles Deleuze, "Literature and Life," trans. Daniel Smith, *Critical Inquiry* 23.2 (1997), p. 225.

79. Ibid.

80. I borrow this phrase, with slight changes, from Laruelle. In his book *Mystique non-philosophique à l'usage des contemporains*, Laruelle discusses the immanent type of mysticism represented in the works of Eckhart, described as a "Vécu-sans-Vie" (Lived-without-Life).

81. Bachelard, *Lautréamont*, p. 55.

82. Georges Bataille, *Theory of Religion*, trans. Robert Hurley (New York: Zone, 1992), p. 34.

83. While eating in horror film may begin in the discontinuity of human beings eating food, it can also open onto the ambiguous continuity of animality, where eater and eaten exist, as Bataille notes, "like water in water." The eaten and the dead come together in horror films that feature tombs and entombment. This is apparent in Expressionist films such as Fritz Lang's *Destiny* (1921), art-horror films such as Carl Theodor Dreyer's *Vampyr* (1932), and in classic Hollywood films such as *Isle of the Dead* (1945). There is also an entire tradition of horror films that depict not the living reminded of death, but the dead coming back to life. Whether it takes place at the individual level, as in *I Walked With A Zombie* (1943), or at the collective level, as in *Revolt of the Zombies* (1936), whether it be via magic, as in *Plague of Zombies* (1966), or via science, as in *The Curse of Frankenstein* (1957), the transformation of life into death implies a minimal, material continuity that is neither life nor death, but that cuts across them both.

84. Bataille, *Theory of Religion*, pp. 50-51.

85. Ibid., p. 35.

86. Ibid., pp. 35-36.

87. Medieval hagiographies such as *The Golden Legend* contain

accounts of cephalophores. For a contemporary account of the cephalophore in relation to horror film, see Nicola Mascandaro's study "Decapitating Cinema," in the collection *And They Were Two In One and One In Two* (London: Schism, 2014).

88. Margheriti, who often directed under the name Anthony Dawson, also directed such low-brow classics as *Castle of Blood, Cannibal Apocalypse,* and the "documentary" *Mondo Inferno.*

89. Lafcadio Hearn, "The Reconciliation," in *Shadowings* (Little, Brown & Company, 1919), pp. 10-11.

90. Another film that deserves mention is a short by John Carpenter titled "The Hair" (featured as part of the 1993 video collection *Body Bags*). In it, a balding man gets a hair transplant but later discovers the true secret to the miracle procedure in the innumerable microscopic worms that are growing out of his scalp.

91. Plato, *Parmenides,* in *The Collected Dialogues of Plato,* ed. Edith Hamilton and Huntington Cairns (Princeton University Press, 1961), 130c-d, p. 924.

92. Pascal, *Pensées,* trans. A.J. Krailsheimer (New York: Penguin, 1966), Fragment #434, p. 165.

93. On Tscherkassky's film, see my chapter "Dark Media," in *Excommunication: Three Inquiries in Media and Mediation,* co-authored with Alexander Galloway and McKenzie Wark (Chicago: University of Chicago Press, 2014), pp. 102ff.

94. Algernon Blackwood, "The Willows," in *Ancient Sorceries and Other Weird Stories,* ed. S.T. Joshi (New York: Penguin, 2002), pp. 56-57.

95. Ibid., p. 57.

96. Ibid., p. 54.

97. Lovecraft, *At the Mountains of Madness,* p. 331.

98. Ibid., p. 334.

99. Ibid., pp. 334-35.

100. Immanuel Kant, *The Critique of Judgement*, trans. James Creed Meredith (Oxford: Clarendon, 1973), §23, p. 90.
101. Ibid., p. 91.
102. Ibid., § 25, p. 98, italics removed. Commenting on the idea of infinity as an example of the sublime, Kant elsewhere notes that "the point of capital importance is that the mere ability even to think it as a *whole* indicates a faculty of mind transcending every standard of sense" (p. 102).
103. Lovecraft, *Supernatural Horror in Literature*, p. 23.
104. Ibid., p. 21.
105. Ibid., p. 23.
106. Lovecraft, "The Shadow Out of Time," in *The Dreams in the Witch-House and Other Weird Stories*, ed. S.T. Joshi (New York: Penguin, 2004), p. 389.
107. Lovecraft, letter to Farnsworth Wright (5 July 1927), *Selected Letters, 1925-1929*, ed. August Derleth and Donald Wandrei (Sauk City: Arkham House, 1968), p. 150.
108. Lovecraft, letter to James Ferdinand Morton (30 October 1929), *Selected Letters, 1929-1931*, ed. August Derleth and Donald Wandrei (Sauk City: Arkham House, 1974), pp. 39ff.
109. For an extended analysis of the "horror" elements in darkness mysticism, see the second volume of this series, *Starry Speculative Corpse*.
110. Dionysius the Areopagite, *The Mystical Theology*, I 1000A, p. 135.
111. Interestingly, with supernatural horror, we find the non-philosophical passage from the *transcendental* (philosophy's condition of knowledge) to the *transcendent* (the non-philosophical limit of all knowledge and experience). But this horrific transcendent remains empty and immanent, a dark unintelligible abyss that is the unhuman.
112. Jun'ichirō Tanizaki, *In Praise of Shadows*, trans. Thomas J. Harper and Edward G. Seidensticker (Stony Creek: Leete's Island Books, 1977), p. 13.

113. Ibid., p. 35.
114. Fyodor Sologub, "Light and Shadow," in *The Dedalus Book of Russian Decadence*, ed. Kirsten Lodge (Sawtry, Cambs: Dedalus, 2007), p. 150.
115. Ibid., p. 155.
116. Ibid., pp. 156-57.
117. Ibid., p. 163.
118. Thomas Ligotti, "The Shadow, the Darkness," in *Teatro Grottesco* (London: Vintage, 2008), p. 259.
119. Ibid., p. 263.
120. Ibid., p. 276.
121. Ibid., pp. 276-77.
122. Victor Stoichita, *A Short History of the Shadow*, trans. Anne-Marie Glasheen (London: Reaktion, 1999), p. 133.
123. Ibid., p. 150.
124. Immanuel Kant, "What Does It Mean To Orient Oneself In Thinking?" (1786), in *Religion and Rational Theology*, ed. and trans. Allen W. Wood (Cambridge: Cambridge University Press, 1996), p. 9.
125. "The Dark," *Lights Out!*, air date 29 December 1937, accessed at http://archive.org.
126. I write about *Uzumaki* in the first volume, *In The Dust of This Planet*, pp. 77ff.
127. Junji Ito, *Uzumaki vol. 3*, trans. Yuji Oniki (San Francisco: Viz Media, 2008), p. 150.
128. Ibid., p. 218.
129. H.P. Lovecraft, "The Unnamable," in *The Dreams in the Witch-House and Other Weird Stories*, ed. S.T. Joshi (New York: Penguin, 2004), p. 89.
130. Iain Hamilton Grant, *Philosophies of Nature After Schelling* (London: Continuum, 2006), p. 169. For an examination of the links between Schelling's philosophy and modern science fiction and horror, see Ben Woodard's *On an Ungrounded Earth: Towards a New Geophilosophy* (Brooklyn:

Punctum, 2013).

131. Ibid., p. 2.

132. Algernon Blackwood, "The Man Whom the Trees Loved," in *Ancient Sorceries and Other Weird Stories*, ed. S.T. Joshi (New York: Penguin, 2002), p. 268, 271.

133. Ibid., p. 268.

134. Izumi Kyōka, "The Holy Man of Mount Kōya," in *Japanese Gothic Tales*, trans. Charles Shirō Inouye (Honolulu: University of Hawaii Press, 1996), pp. 36-37.

135. Ibid., p. 37.

136. Caitlín R. Kiernan, "In the Water Works (Birmingham, Alabama 1888)," in *Tales of Pain and Wonder* (Atlanta: Meisha Merlin Publishing, 2001), p. 294.

137. Ibid., p. 296.

138. Ibid.

139. Fort, *The Book of the Damned: The Collected Works of Charles Fort* (New York: Tarcher/Penguin, 2008), p. 9.

140. Ibid., p. 13.

141. Ibid., p. 14.

142. Ibid.

143. China Miéville, *Kraken* (London: Pan Books, 2011), p. 417.

144. Ibid., p. 186.

145. Ibid., p. 106. The passage is adapted from Rondelet's 15th century teratology treatise *Crinis Abyssi*.

146. Ibid., p. 295.

147. Ambroise Paré, *On Monsters and Marvels*, trans. Janis L. Pallister (Chicago: University of Chicago Press, 1982), p. 161.

148. Vilém Flusser and Louis Bec, *Vampyroteuthis Infernalis: A Treatise, with a Report by the Institut Scientifique de Recherche Paranaturaliste*, trans. Valentine A. Pakis (Minneapolis: University of Minnesota Press, 2012), p. 6.

149. Ibid., p. 11.

150. Ibid.

151. H.P. Lovecraft, "Dagon," in *The Call of Cthulhu and Other Weird Stories*, ed. S.T. Joshi (New York: Penguin, 1999), pp. 1-2.

152. Ibid., p. 2.

153. Ibid., p. 6.

154. Ligotti, *The Conspiracy Against the Human Race*, pp. 52, 101.

155. Ibid., p. 104.

156. Ibid., p. 16. The literary theorist Tzevtan Todorov has provided what is still the classic study on this phenomenon in his book *The Fantastic*.

157. For more on the notion of concept-horror see the journal *Collapse*, volume IV (2008): http://www.urbanomic.com /pub_collapse4.php.

158. Ligotti, *Conspiracy*, pp. 220, 221

159. Quoted in Ligotti, *Conspiracy*, p. 37, from Mainländer's main philosophical work, *Die Philosophie der Erlösung* (*The Philosophy of Redemption*).

160. Ligotti, *Conspiracy*, p. 28.

161. Ibid., p. 27.

162. We might also include, in this list of "self-help" pessimists, John Gray's *Straw Dogs*, a provocation-for-the-sake-of-provocation, Roger Scruton's conservative and bland *The Uses of Pessimism*, and Alain de Botton's naive and patronizing *Religion for Atheists*, all of which argue in favor of the healthy side-effects of pessimist thinking.

163. Ligotti, *Conspiracy*, p. 16.

164. Ibid., p. 17.

165. Ibid., pp. 51-52.

166. It is tempting to include others under this rubric of ecstatic pessimism, though they would most likely refuse such a label: Ray Brassier, who also provides the Foreword to *Conspiracy*, and whose work (e.g. *Nihil Unbound*) uniquely engages with the philosophy of science; Reza Negarestani, whose work (e.g. "The Non-Trivial Goat") charts a path

between horror and mathematics; and my own recent writing ("Cosmic Pessimism"), which has been increasingly drawn to the aphorism and the fragment.

167. Ligotti, "The Puppet Masters," in *Noctuary* (New York: Carroll & Graf, 1995), p. 172.

168. Guibert of Nogent, *A Monk's Confession*, trans. Paul Archamabult (University Park: Penn State University Press, 2006), pp. 51-52.

169. Immanuel Kant, *The Critique of Judgement*, §25, pp. 94, 97.

170. Ibid., §28, pp. 110-11.

171. Ibid., §28, p. 111; "General Remark," p. 120.

172. Ibid., "General Remark," p. 120.

173. Ibid., §26, p. 103, italics removed.

174. Ibid., "General Remark," p. 131.

175. Rudolf Otto, *The Idea of the Holy*, p. 28.

176. Devendra Varma, *The Gothic Flame* (New York: Russell & Russell, 1957), p. 211.

177. Ibid.

178. S.L. Varnado, *Haunted Presence: The Numinous in Gothic Fiction* (Tuscaloosa: University of Alabama Press, 1987), p. 17.

179. Denys Turner, *The Darkness of God: Negativity in Christian Mysticism* (Cambridge: Cambridge University Press, 1999), p. 264.

180. Ibid., p. 35.

181. Cf. Suzanne Guerlac, *The Impersonal Sublime: Hugo, Baudelaire, Lautréamont* (Stanford: Stanford University Press, 1990), pp. 185ff.

182. Immanuel Kant, *Critique of Pure Reason*, trans. Norman Kemp Smith (New York: St. Martin's, 1964), p. 259.

183. Caroline Walker Bynum, *Christian Materiality: An Essay on Religion in Late Medieval Europe* (New York: Zone, 2011), p. 17.

184. Ibid., p. 20.

185. Ibid., p. 31.

186. Ibid.

187. Raymond of Capua, *The Life of St. Catherine of Siena*, trans. George Lamb (Ann Arbor: Harvill Press, 1960), p. 43.

188. Thomas Frognall Dibdin, *The Bibliomania; or, Book-Madness; Containing Some Account of the History, Symptoms, and Cure of this Fatal Disease* (London: Longman, Hurst, Rees, and Orme, 1809), p. 58.

Contemporary culture has eliminated both the concept of the public and the figure of the intellectual. Former public spaces – both physical and cultural – are now either derelict or colonized by advertising. A cretinous anti-intellectualism presides, cheerled by expensively educated hacks in the pay of multinational corporations who reassure their bored readers that there is no need to rouse themselves from their interpassive stupor. The informal censorship internalized and propagated by the cultural workers of late capitalism generates a banal conformity that the propaganda chiefs of Stalinism could only ever have dreamt of imposing. Zer0 Books knows that another kind of discourse – intellectual without being academic, popular without being populist – is not only possible: it is already flourishing, in the regions beyond the striplit malls of so-called mass media and the neurotically bureaucratic halls of the academy. Zer0 is committed to the idea of publishing as a making public of the intellectual. It is convinced that in the unthinking, blandly consensual culture in which we live, critical and engaged theoretical reflection is more important than ever before.

ZERO BOOKS

If this book has helped you to clarify an idea, solve a problem or extend your knowledge, you may like to read more titles from Zero Books. Recent bestsellers are:

Capitalist Realism Is there no alternative?
Mark Fisher
An analysis of the ways in which capitalism has presented itself as the only realistic political-economic system.
Paperback: November 27, 2009 978-1-84694-317-1 $14.95 £7.99.
eBook: July 1, 2012 978-1-78099-734-6 $9.99 £6.99.

The Wandering Who? A study of Jewish identity politics
Gilad Atzmon
An explosive unique crucial book tackling the issues of Jewish Identity Politics and ideology and their global influence.
Paperback: September 30, 2011 978-1-84694-875-6 $14.95 £8.99.
eBook: September 30, 2011 978-1-84694-876-3 $9.99 £6.99.

Clampdown Pop-cultural wars on class and gender
Rhian E. Jones
Class and gender in Britpop and after, and why 'chav' is a feminist issue.
Paperback: March 29, 2013 978-1-78099-708-7 $14.95 £9.99.
eBook: March 29, 2013 978-1-78099-707-0 $7.99 £4.99.

The Quadruple Object
Graham Harman
Uses a pack of playing cards to present Harman's metaphysical system of fourfold objects, including human access, Heidegger's indirect causation, panpsychism and ontography.
Paperback: July 29, 2011 978-1-84694-700-1 $16.95 £9.99.

Weird Realism Lovecraft and Philosophy
Graham Harman
As Hölderlin was to Martin Heidegger and Mallarmé to Jacques
Derrida, so is H.P. Lovecraft to the Speculative Realist philoso-
phers.
Paperback: September 28, 2012 978-1-78099-252-5 $24.95 £14.99.
eBook: September 28, 2012 978-1-78099-907-4 $9.99 £6.99.

Sweetening the Pill or How We Got Hooked on Hormonal Birth
Control
Holly Grigg-Spall
Is it really true? Has contraception liberated or oppressed
women?
Paperback: September 27, 2013 978-1-78099-607-3 $22.95 £12.99.
eBook: September 27, 2013 978-1-78099-608-0 $9.99 £6.99.

Why Are We The Good Guys? Reclaiming Your Mind From The
Delusions Of Propaganda
David Cromwell
A provocative challenge to the standard ideology that Western
power is a benevolent force in the world.
Paperback: September 28, 2012 978-1-78099-365-2 $26.95 £15.99.
eBook: September 28, 2012 978-1-78099-366-9 $9.99 £6.99.

The Truth about Art Reclaiming quality
Patrick Doorly
The book traces the multiple meanings of art to their various
sources, and equips the reader to choose between them.
Paperback: August 30, 2013 978-1-78099-841-1 $32.95 £19.99.

Bells and Whistles More Speculative Realism
Graham Harman
In this diverse collection of sixteen essays, lectures, and inter-
views Graham Harman lucidly explains the principles of

Speculative Realism, including his own object-oriented philosophy.
Paperback: November 29, 2013 978-1-78279-038-9 $26.95 £15.99.
eBook: November 29, 2013 978-1-78279-037-2 $9.99 £6.99.

Towards Speculative Realism: Essays and Lectures Essays and Lectures
Graham Harman
These writings chart Harman's rise from Chicago sportswriter to co founder of one of Europe's most promising philosophical movements: Speculative Realism.
Paperback: November 26, 2010 978-1-84694-394-2 $16.95 £9.99.
eBook: January 1, 1970 978-1-84694-603-5 $9.99 £6.99.

Meat Market Female flesh under capitalism
Laurie Penny
A feminist dissection of women's bodies as the fleshy fulcrum of capitalist cannibalism, whereby women are both consumers and consumed.
Paperback: April 29, 2011 978-1-84694-521-2 $12.95 £6.99.
eBook: May 21, 2012 978-1-84694-782-7 $9.99 £6.99.

Translating Anarchy The Anarchism of Occupy Wall Street
Mark Bray
An insider's account of the anarchists who ignited Occupy Wall Street.
Paperback: September 27, 2013 978-1-78279-126-3 $26.95 £15.99.
eBook: September 27, 2013 978-1-78279-125-6 $6.99 £4.99.

One Dimensional Woman
Nina Power
Exposes the dark heart of contemporary cultural life by examining pornography, consumer capitalism and the ideology of women's work.

Paperback: November 27, 2009 978-1-84694-241-9 $14.95 £7.99.
eBook: July 1, 2012 978-1-78099-737-7 $9.99 £6.99.

Dead Man Working
Carl Cederstrom, Peter Fleming
An analysis of the dead man working and the way in which
capital is now colonizing life itself.
Paperback: May 25, 2012 978-1-78099-156-6 $14.95 £9.99.
eBook: June 27, 2012 978-1-78099-157-3 $9.99 £6.99.

Unpatriotic History of the Second World War
James Heartfield
The Second World War was not the Good War of legend. James
Heartfield explains that both Allies and Axis powers fought for
the same goals - territory, markets and natural resources.
Paperback: September 28, 2012 978-1-78099-378-2 $42.95 £23.99.
eBook: September 28, 2012 978-1-78099-379-9 $9.99 £6.99.

Find more titles at www.zero-books.net